UN

Overcome Distraction,
Build Healthy Digital Habits and
Use Tech to Create a Life You Love

TETHERED

SINI NINKOVIC

UNTETHERED

First published by Sini Ninkovic 2021

Copyright © 2021 Sini Ninkovic.

ISBN: 9798473055993

To my grandpa Mladjen, who passed away the week I finished writing this book. He somehow managed to never pick up my WhatsApp calls. When he called me, he hardly understood a word I was saying. And still he helped me understand the immense value of personal relationships.

CONTENTS

Overdependence or Addiction?
What Does Being Untethered Entail?
My Kryptonite
Untethered: A Guide to Creating a Healthy
Relationship with Digital Technologies

Trend #1: Increasing Complexity
Trend #2: Negative Media Bias
Trend #3: Extractive Algorithms
Trend #4: Abundance of Choice
Trend #5: Convenience Economy
Understanding the Trends

Upgrade #1: Tackling the True Source of Negativity
Upgrade #2: Committing to Responsibility, Curiosity and Your Powers
Upgrade #3: Understanding Our Purpose
Upgrade #4: Reconnecting to Future You
Commitments to Yourself

PREFACE

The year 2017 kicked off a difficult three-year period for me. For the first time in my career, I was struggling to do my job well. I started to feel purposeless and depressed.

I asked friends for advice and tried many new experiences, thinking models, tools, and ways of expressing myself to overcome these struggles, but nothing seemed to really work. Gosh, I left my job, tried out #vanlife, read self-help books and so much more in an attempt to regain joy and fulfillment. Even working with a therapist every week didn't seem to truly change the way I felt about myself. Objectively, there was nothing wrong. I was earning good money, I had friends that I liked, and my relationship was going well.

Then one of my friends recommended trying out a ten-day silent meditation retreat under the S.N. Goenka tradition in Northern California. It was one of the best decisions of my life. I came out of this unique experience with a deeper understanding of myself and glimpses of what I was supposed to do next. I wanted to help myself and others reclaim their purpose and find new levels of fulfillment.

That desire eventually led me to write this book, or some version of it. By May 2020 I had completed my research and written 110,000 words, then cut them in half to create the first draft of a book called LIT. I wrote most of it during a sixty-day challenge I'd set for myself and followed through on with a couple responsibility buddies. I even sent the book to an editor for review and got some encouraging feedback.

Then, I decided not to publish it. In fact, I felt ashamed. Although the advice in the book was useful and valid, I had not managed to use it to find happiness or feel more fulfilled myself. It became clear that I was missing something, some part of the equation to a happier life. It felt like I knew what I should be doing, but I still wasn't taking my own advice. But why?

I spent a couple of weeks reflecting on what I'd learned writing LIT. I wondered if I'd missed anything major in the book. I talked about the value of different mental health and spiritual practices and how our mind can play tricks on us. I described mindset changes that can lead to a healthier relationship with ourselves. I talked about other books, and even brought in my own struggles. But still it felt like there was something missing.

I wondered, was there a common thread, something I'd been doing consistently throughout my life or at least the past several years that was holding me back? I wrote about it in my journal, discussed it with friends, and researched it online. After some time, and endless hours digging through memories of unhappy moments, it became clear that the obstacle was right in front of me. It had been there every day for most of my life, gaining power slowly.

It wasn't my job or the people I surrounded myself with. I thought I needed to meditate more (which is still true), or that I was missing a regimented morning routine. It wasn't about how often I played sports each week or where I was living. All of these things can have effects on our well-being, but they weren't the main contributors to my depression and lack of fulfillment. There was one constant, at all times, hiding in plain sight.

My smartphone.

In some ways, my smartphone had become my kryptonite over the years. What seemed so useful in the beginning increasingly became a source of distraction and instant gratification, affecting my mental health. It was also the thing I spent most of my time with. What irony. In hindsight, I'd always felt that there was something unhealthy about the way I used my phone, but I'd normalized my experience by seeing others behave in similar ways without seeing them struggling with their own mental health.

Of course, it wasn't my smartphone per se. The smartphone just stood for a bigger issue: the way I was relating to digital technologies. I had not created a healthy relationship with my devices, but rather engaged in toxic behaviors every day, gaming deep into the night, binge watching, and unconsciously scrolling my time away.

I didn't realize it back then, but like so many, I had a dependent relationship with my smartphone that had turned toxic as my phone became more powerful. While the time spent on my phone was increasing every year, it did not seem like my conscious time spent with the device was increasing. A lot of it simply felt lost in a void of black mirrors.

I knew that I had to figure out how to improve my relationship with my smartphone. What I didn't know was that getting my relationship with tech right would be the most impactful thing I'd ever do for my well-being, success, and happiness.

Once I figured out what worked and what didn't, I started writing *Untethered*. The book became my guide to creating a lifestyle that has helped me unlock healthy digital habits, focus attention on what matters to me, and nourish my relationship with my digital devices and, ultimately, with myself.

* * *

The reality of the twenty-first century is that we—at least most of us—will need our devices to survive and thrive. Most of us won't be able to just dispose of our smartphones and get a dumbphone without significantly disadvantaging ourselves in many ways. And I don't believe that we need to. The secret to unlocking your best future is to create a functioning relationship with technology that helps you be your fullest, happiest self.

In the two years before publishing this book, I tried out different routines, read endless books on digital minimalism and digital wellness, consulted with researchers and thought leaders, became a licensed Digital Wellness Educator,1 and ultimately redesigned how I lived my life from the ground up with the understanding that I would always have my smartphone by my side.

And I know that you can do the same—create more awareness, more fulfillment, and a better understanding of yourself—with your devices by your side instead of believing that pushing them away will create the life you desire. But before I dive into how you can unlock your powers alongside your devices instead of being hypnotized by them, I want to acknowledge two things.

First, if you are struggling with depression or serious addictions, you should consult a mental health practitioner. One of the most important steps in my journey toward a healthy relationship with myself was engaging with a therapist. The weekly sessions helped me better understand and contextualize my situation before I was able to test and implement strategies to improve my relationship with tech. This book cannot replace mental health practitioners when it comes to serious illnesses.

Second, the debate over new technologies, like digital devices, is not actually new. Throughout history, the introduction of influential technologies has been the subject of much debate and blame. A great example is the debate over what today is at the core of communication: the written word. Some believed that the overdependence on writing and reading would change a person's mind by replacing their memories with words, make us shallower thinkers and less intellectual, and even prevent us from achieving true happiness.2 If you haven't yet, I am sure you will hear many (incl. myself at times) claim that digital tech might be doing the same to us.

There is evidence that our interaction with the internet is altering our brains. But there is also evidence that most habits and routines will do that, too. The question is not whether the things we do and consume will affect our brains, but rather how they will and how we can turn them into positive influences. The how, I believe, depends on our ways of relating with technology and using the devices in our lives. Everything can become a poison when used in the wrong quantities or ways.

Untethered is a book that encourages and guides you to take regular actions that improve how you relate to your digital devices and to yourself. I believe that it will help you live a fuller life with technology supporting your journey rather than holding you back from it. And if after reading the book you want to dive even deeper, visit TheUntetheredBook.com, where you'll find more information and challenges to transform your life without giving up on technology altogether.

I hope that what I've learned on my journey, now distilled into this book, can help you create the life you desire with the help of humanity's most powerful tool in your hand.

FREE GUIDE

In addition to this book, readers can download a **free, 20-page guide containing 3 clever tricks to master your digital attention**.

Just go to theuntetheredbook.com to get your free guide.

ACKNOWLEDGEMENTS

I've done many things in my life where I thought, "This might be the hardest project I have taken on yet." Everything from taking on working on electric cars at BMW, moving by myself to the US, getting into the UC Berkeley Haas School of Business, getting a job at Apple and launching several Mac computer lines, to living in a camper van and doing a ten-day silent vipassanā meditation retreat. Writing a book might just be the hardest piece of work I have taken on yet.

If I hadn't actively asked for and received help from some incredible people, this dream of mine would have likely failed early on. I want to first thank the people who have actually helped me grow into somebody who is able to ask for help and knows some of his limitations. I'm eternally grateful to my parents, whom I typically refer to as the most incredible, humble, and considerate human being I've ever met. I know that to be a fact because many of my friends have said similar things about them. I am proud of who they are, how they have developed and grown over the years, and how much trust they have in me. They didn't complain when I told them that I would quit my job at arguably the most successful company in the world, nor did they resist my invitation to join me at Burning Man in 2019, which was one of the highlights of my life.

I want to thank my sister Marijana, who helped me develop a stronger connection to my heart. Her encouragement and love have always helped me go farther than I could have without the feeling of being supported. She has also taught me that we are all individuals, significantly different from each other even when we enjoy the same upbringing.

Although the last few years of my life have been filled with many ups and downs, my friend and partner Emily stood by me and supported me through all of them. Never would I have had the guts to follow my dreams if it hadn't been for her nudging me toward my potential. She is responsible for much of the growth I went through in the last few years and has never stopped believing in me. I am deeply grateful for the most crucial lessons of my adult life, the fun and laughter, and the sadness and struggle we have gone through together.

A special thanks goes out to my European friends and family who have supported me from afar. I am often in awe at the fact that no matter how many years pass and how long I'm away from them, every time I come back they welcome me like I've never left, like I am still part of their closest family. Knowing that I can come back and still be welcomed with that much love keeps me going when things are hard.

Writing a book about something as important as our relationship with technology and sharing my own life in it is an unreal process. It could have never been completed without all the friends and colleagues who helped me on this path. First and foremost, I want to thank Ray Sylvester, my main editor and collaborator on this book. The first time we spoke was a year before the publication of this book. We started to work together about six months later, and I couldn't be happier that we did. Not only did you do the job of an editor, you named the book, proposed major directional changes, and were the sanity check on all my crazy ideas throughout. Your commitment, resilience, and steady demeanor have made it one of the easiest and most fruitful collaborations of my life.

I want to thank Ryan Bush, who has inspired me by successfully self-publishing his own book Designing the Mind. Besides having read my book a couple of times and providing me with valuable feedback, you have also been the creative director of the *Untethered* family, created the artwork, and led some of the publishing efforts. Your many abilities allowed you to fill multiple roles and I couldn't imagine this achievement without you.

My first editor, Jeff Shreve, who gave me feedback on my first book LIT, helped lay the foundation for the changes that led to *Untethered*. Without his feedback, I would not have had the understanding about the strengths and weaknesses of my writing style and content. He nudged me to develop my style and change the content in a direction that ultimately led to this book.

I want to thank the three accountability buddies who helped me the most on this book writing journey: my friends Kim, Dan, and David. Kim has inspired me to become a better and more thoughtful writer. I learned so much from your meticulous approach, and I am eternally grateful for those lessons. Dan and I spent between two and four hours every weekday together over a four-month period. You helped me through the most difficult part of this journey, refining my message and making sure that my voice came through during the peak of the coronavirus crisis. And David, thank you for recently joining me as daily accountability support. The ease you bring to every situation makes me feel at home, heard, and easily understood. Thank you for making sure I stay on track with my commitments.

Thank you Sea Sloat, Michaela Carmein, and Valerie Beltran for first of all being great friends but also being willing to review my book and give me early feedback. Sea, thank you for the short stint we spent editing the book together. Your ideas and vision of the world have inspired me to not only become a better writer but also to come out with a book that feels more aligned with my inner voice. And Michaela, thank you, for so many different teachings, for your humble and warm ways of communicating, and also for your ability to spark true creativity. You are such a truly beautiful soul. Valerie, you are such an inspiration and one of my closest friends. You make me a better person, and your trust in me warms my heart, whether we are in the same city or on the other side of the world.

I want to also thank my San Francisco Bay Area community. You are incredibly special people, the most unique bunch I have ever met. There is a reason why so many of you are or will be making unimaginable changes in this world. I am proud to know you, and I am happy to call many of you family. Thank you for your ongoing support. No matter where in the world I am or where in the world many of you end up being, I feel the connection every time we are in conversation. You will always be representative of the unique spirit that one can only truly experience in the Bay Area.

And finally, I want to thank my digital devices and the internet. Most of what I know today, I learned through you. I am grateful for the information you make available to me every day and your ability to be there whenever I need you for connection and communication.

INTRODUCTION: OUR RELATIONSHIP WITH TECHNOLOGY

I have a friend who decided, after a lifetime of sobriety, to experiment with alcohol. After decades as a committed member of the Mormon Church, Adam (not his real name) wanted to try something that was taboo in his community yet normal for most Americans. He was ready to step into the unknown and explore this mind-altering substance for the first time.

What changed, you might ask? In his early thirties, Adam had started to question the belief system of his church. He thought that trying alcohol might help him better comprehend the rationale behind banning it and revitalize his belief in Mormonism.

Adam had never been to a bar or liquor store. He didn't know what types of liquor existed. He'd never heard his family or friends talk about how to mix a good drink. He didn't even know that many alcoholic drinks were mixed to begin with.

So he drove for forty-five minutes until he reached a liquor store far from his community. He asked one of the store's employees for recommendations, which he followed: whiskey, bourbon, vodka, absinth, and of course, tequila. He didn't ask for mixers, and the employee didn't recommend any, assuming Adam would know how to drink.

Back home, Adam poured himself a glass of vodka—straight, no ice—and started sipping it like water. Five minutes later, he'd finished the glass. Another fifteen minutes later, he was tipsy. For the first time in his life, Adam was experiencing an altered state of mind!

Adam enjoyed the new perspective alcohol was providing him with and decided to continue experimenting with different types of alcohol for a few weeks. Glass after glass, he chugged them like lemonade while trying to hide his experimentation from his wife and kids. Some of the tastes he enjoyed, while others disgusted him, but either way, the newfound state of mind was exciting.

Suffice it to say, Adam had no idea what he was doing. And how could he have? His education and upbringing hadn't included the lessons that most American college kids, and even high schoolers, typically experience at a young age. Nobody in his community knew what drinking responsibly even meant. At the end of the day, he became a husband and father of two children before he'd had his first glass of alcohol!

About a month into the experiment, after a grueling day at work at a tech startup, Adam's colleagues suggested drinks. They invited Adam, although mostly out of courtesy, knowing that he'd declined their offers in the past. But this time Adam was ready, and he told them he would join, for just one drink.

Adam had never been to a bar or ordered a drink before, and boy, was he excited! The bar atmosphere, the loud chatter, the cool bartenders mixing up drinks...all of this was new to him.

Because it was his first time, he let his friends order a drink for him: a gin and tonic. Adam watched the bartender with fascination as he mixed the group's drinks. He enjoyed the bartender's fancy moves and handling of glasses but he was disappointed with the result. Adam noticed the bartender poured just a tiny sip of alcohol into the glass before filling the rest with tonic water. He couldn't believe what was happening. "Fifteen dollars for tonic water with a tiny bit of gin? Outrageous."

So Adam asked his colleagues, "Are we getting screwed over? Why did the bartender pour so little alcohol?" His colleagues stared at each other in confusion, but realizing this was new to Adam explained it was a normal mixed-drink ratio. Hard liquor was supposed to be drunk responsibly, in small quantities!

That day, during his first ever social drinking experience, Adam was shocked and a little embarrassed to find out that drinking an entire glass full of hard liquor wasn't normal or healthy. Adam realized that he had been an uneducated drinker, getting wasted at home every other night without knowing. His family and friends never drank and alcohol was not part of the culture, so how could he have known any differently?

* * *

The crazy thing is that in some way, we're all like Adam, at least when it comes to our smartphones and other digital technologies. We consume information and media every day with little awareness or regard to the consequences to our well-being. Digital technology is so new and evolving so rapidly that it's hard to know how exactly it's influencing us. Should we be allowed to drive if we spend an entire day scrolling through Facebook or binge watching Netflix?

Digital technologies can easily overwhelm us with complexity, choice and conveniences. They have access to our own design flaws and human weaknesses and often understand us better than we understand ourselves. Tech has the power to influence our behaviors every single day.

If you've seen The Social Dilemma on Netflix, you know what I'm talking about. In this documentary—which was seen by over forty million households within two months of release and took only three weeks to become Netflix's most popular documentary of 2020—tech experts came together to sound the alarm on the dangers of social networking and smartphones.

Like many others, I have started to feel that something might be wrong or even unhealthy with the way we're using our devices. What started as innocent tools have become the most powerful machines mankind has ever held in its hands. So powerful that it sometimes feels like we lose control of them or even lose ourselves in them.

Most of us are familiar with what it feels like to spend more time on our smartphones than we'd like. Even my sixty-year-old mother has experienced this sense of defeat. We've all spent a long day staring at our screens, checking social media and streaming sites like TikTok, Facebook, Instagram, and YouTube, or playing mobile games. We take a few breaks to do things humans have to do, like eat food, take a shower, and brush our teeth. Other than that, sometimes it feels as if every moment is spent consuming media.

But every now and then, for a few minutes or just a second, we end up listening more deeply to ourselves. When we're not distracted by work, friends, or our phones, we get the sense that some of our tech usage is no longer contributing to our progress or well-being. We feel busy, constantly doing things while besieged by the nagging sense that there's hardly any time to get shit done. We feel like we are in constant motion, yet we don't arrive anywhere. We feel stuck in a cycle of constant distraction by our phone, smart watch, laptop, TV, or iPad.

If you have experienced this defeated feeling, you are not alone with the sadness, anxiety, and distraction these black mirrors can invoke. And this experience is also becoming more common every single year!

U.S. adults spend 11 hours and 27 minutes per day connected to media" - Nielsen Research, 2019[3]

"U.S. adults spend 12 hours and 21 minutes per day connected to media" - Nielsen Research, 2020[4]

The truth is that American adults spend more than half of their hours consuming media, including TV, radio, computer, smartphone, and video game content. If we account for sleep, which averages to 6.8 hours per night in the US, we end up consuming media for two thirds of our waking life. That means the average American spends about 2.5 times more time connected than engaged with the real world.

Typically, when we do something often, we develop healthy behaviors around it over time. Let's take sleep, for example. We invest in comfortable mattresses, listen to soothing music before bed, have plush teddies to cuddle, enjoy weighted blankets, put on sleeping masks, and use alarm clocks—all to help us get higher quality sleep in fewer hours.

Needless to say, many of us have not yet developed a healthy relationship with our internet-enabled devices, especially our smartphones. The tentacles of these devices crept in over the past decade, taking up more space in our lives every year. This is not surprising, because our technology provides us with powers that would have been considered magical just two generations ago. I can't imagine a life without my smartphone anymore. Tech has had—and I will talk about this more in future chapters—an overwhelmingly positive influence on us. But many tech devices have also been downgrading some of our core human capabilities, negatively affecting our ability to focus, be patient, and resist urges.

Internet-enabled devices allow us to be physically present but mentally absent and often make it more uncomfortable to be mentally available. Why else do we replace any moment of boredom with the comfort of unlocking our phones? Why else would young adults be distracting themselves by checking their phones 150-plus times per day?[5]

In 2020, with the coronavirus forcing us to spend more time at home, our technology consumption increased dramatically. From 2019 to 2020, our smartphone use alone increased by forty-five minutes! We seem to prioritize our relationships with our smartphones over those with other humans. Considering that we only spend 2.5 hours per day with our significant others and that this time is decreasing every year, it seems pretty clear which relationship takes priority.

I now believe that many of us are unaware of the influence that tech has on our lives. And, even though we all experience the lows after a long day of scrolling on our phones, most haven't acknowledged their dependence on their portals to endless consumption.

With alcohol, most people (maybe not Adam) know how much they can consume and still drive safely. But most of us probably don't know how much technology we can consume before it's no longer safe to drive or go outside at all. Nobody tells us how much Instagramming is too much, or what the negative consequences of online gaming on our long-term health are, or what watching hours of YouTube content can do to our mental well-being.

Not only do we not understand how to evaluate our online consumption (it would be great if we had something like calories to evaluate food or promille to measure blood alcohol levels), we also consume content from creators who capitalize on this absence of healthy habits. They desire our time and attention. The ones who get our attention typically scream the loudest. And parents only know to tell us that we shouldn't play for too long, or to put down our phones at dinner. But how trustworthy is that guidance when they use their phones for hours every day without restrictions?

Most Americans are drinking glassfuls of online content every single day without understanding the long-term risks of their behavior. Unfortunately, those risks are not obvious. They're hidden deep in the algorithms that drive popular social media sites, obscured by the variety of choice that comes with every Amazon search, and concealed from the public eye through beautiful interfaces.

So, it makes sense that tech companies are so unforthcoming about their secret sauce. That sauce, one could argue, is the creation of some kind of dependency. This shouldn't be news. Tech companies, like any for-profit institution, want their customers to become attached to them. They crave your attention and whether you give it consciously or unconsciously doesn't really matter, because attention has become the most valuable currency in the world. At the end of the day, you pay for the internet by being online.

OVERDEPENDENCE OR ADDICTION?

Before I share with you how gaming has affected my teenage years and early adulthood, I want to address a common misconception that you might be wondering about as well: is technology actually addictive, habit forming, or programmed to keep humans engaged? It's clear that we spend a lot of time in the digital world, but does that automatically make us digital addicts?

People who overuse technology may develop similar brain chemistry and neural patterns to those who are addicted to various substances.[6] In one study that confirmed this evaluation, researchers scanned the brains of young people with internet addiction disorder (IAD) and found them to be similar to those of people with substance addictions to alcohol, cocaine, and cannabis.[7]

But what is even more concerning is that smartphones seem to serve as an effective gateway drug. A study by the UK National Health Service found that teens who texted frequently were 40 percent more likely to have used cigarettes and twice as likely to have used alcohol as students who were less frequent users of technology.[8] The study also suggests that kids who spent more hours per school day on social networks were at higher risk for depression and suicide.

Another 2019 European study not only confirmed that higher smartphone usage is correlated with lower levels of well-being, life satisfaction, and mindfulness, it also determined that levels of well-being are a predictor of smartphone usage![9] It seems that when people are unhappy with their life circumstances, they are more likely to escape into the digital realm, which makes them even unhappier.

"The cascade of neuroprocesses that kicks off the brain's reward circuitry and the rush of the pleasure chemical dopamine can be triggered just as easily by the release of the latest iPhone as by alcohol, sex, or a fast car. In some ways, technology is a drug."

- **Nutt and Jensen**, 2015[10]

In summary, internet addiction disorder changes our brains and smartphone overuse makes us more likely to escape into the digital realm or consume other substances. But, and I think this is extremely important to understand, technology doesn't seem to be more addictive than any other substance or activity that generates highs. Everything that produces highs can be overused and can become addictive. As Nir Eyal, the author of Hooked and Indistractable—and who has years of experience researching technology dependency—once told me, "Everything rewarding engages the reward systems in the brain." Technology use sure is rewarding!

Smartphones and technology in general—at least in the ways we use them today—might be hampering our well-being and making it harder for us to escape negative states by reinforcing their use. It's a vicious cycle: the ways we use our smartphones might instill worse habits in us.

"Highs also generate addiction. The more you rely on them to feel better about your underlying problems, the more you will seek them out. In this sense, almost anything can become addictive, depending on the motivation behind using it."

- **Mark Manson**, The Subtle Art of Not Giving A F*

Admittedly, some of this sounds scary, and there's apparently a simple conclusion to draw here: tech is bad for our well-being, and we should limit its influence on us. Scientists say it can affect us negatively, our daily experiences prove that we often end up hypnotized by tech, and now a major Netflix documentary with some big-name tech leaders claims that tech algorithms can be harmful. Our digital technologies, especially our smartphones, seem to be preventing many of us from living fulfilled and happy lives. Maybe the government should step in and regulate digital technologies and the algorithms behind them more carefully?

I believe that regulating tech companies is one means of reducing our overconsumption. Unfortunately, regulating tech is hard to get right considering how complex and wide reaching technologies have become. It's worth trying but will likely take time. But what if instead of waiting for regulation to kick in or believing technology to be inherently bad, we took responsibility for managing our powerful and ever-available devices for our greatest good/benefit? We need to take responsibility.

We developed humanity's most powerful tool by creating the internet and connecting it to a device that you can carry with you at all times, the smartphone. Want a new romantic partner? Download a dating app. Want groceries, or even better, restaurant food delivered within minutes to your door? Try Uber Eats or Instacart. Want a new piece of hardware? Just order it through Amazon. No need to leave your home! These apps would have been considered magic just a century ago.

With the internet, it's like we copied our own neural network, created a new one that connects all of us, and made it available to everyone through a small screen. And with the smartphone we basically created the one ring to rule them all.

With great power comes great responsibility, and smartphones are no different; their power can be overwhelming when they are not used responsibly. Most of us have experienced this in some way at some point. Smartphones can cause a loss of reality, dependency and disconnection from others when used to escape reality. Sometimes I wish I had been given more guidance on how to use my devices responsibly. Just let this sink in for a moment: Isn't it absurd that our most powerful and captivating tool, the iPhone, comes with the shortest possible instruction manual?

"Digital technologies are not necessarily more addictive than other tools, experiences or substances but they are influencing society on a much larger scale."

- **Damian Tew**, neuroscientist and former program manager at Google

Some of Silicon Valley's tech leaders understand that there are real negative consequences to their creations and thus desire regulation. And, I am sure that regulation can reduce some of the problems if introduced thoughtfully. But whether you believe that we should establish more oversight mechanisms for tech companies, moderate online content, or introduce ID verification for children on the internet, that isn't really the point, at least not in this book.

I believe personal change has to come from within. No matter how technology might be regulated in future, regulation is not going to cover every corner of the internet, with all the loopholes it provides. And regulation wouldn't resolve the real issue at hand. We are getting distracted from our own needs and long-term desires. We are holding ourselves back from fulfillment by getting stuck in repetitive media consumption cycles. And much like the prohibition of alcohol in the US in the 1920s, overregulation can backfire.

Just one hundred years ago, alcohol sales were banned nationwide. Leaders in the temperance/prohibition movement of the nineteenth and early twentieth century emphasized alcohol's negative effects on people's health, personalities, and family lives and demanded limiting its availability, which led to national prohibitions in Canada, the US, and Norway. But the problem of people overconsuming alcohol wasn't resolved by banning alcohol sales; it made people desire alcoholic beverages more!

Let me put it in the famous words of John D. Rockefeller, Jr., who initially supported Prohibition in the US:

"When Prohibition was introduced, I hoped ... the day would soon come when the evil effects of alcohol would be recognized. I have slowly and reluctantly come to believe that this has not been the result. Instead, drinking has generally increased; the speakeasy has replaced the saloon; a vast army of lawbreakers has appeared; many of our best citizens have openly ignored Prohibition; respect for the law has been greatly lessened; and crime has increased to a level never seen before."

We are responsible for our own consumption patterns, whether they're related to alcohol or technology. Over time most of us develop a healthy relationship with alcohol, so why couldn't we do the same with our smartphones? Regulation can help us, but at the end of the day, each of us is responsible for making the changes we desire. The one thing we have immediate control over is our own actions, even if they are influenced by tech companies. Blaming big tech is an easy way out of that responsibility and a direct path into more misery.

There are great examples in other countries of how increasing education and support systems instead of regulation can lead to a desirable outcome. In 2001, Portugal decriminalized the use of all illicit drugs. Instead of banning and punishing, they offered education and rehab centers nationwide. Substance abuse and addiction issues are handled by advisors, psychologists, and social workers instead of police and prison officers. As a result, substance abuse and dependence was cut in half. And the US might finally follow this example: as of February 2021, the state of Oregon has decriminalized drugs and offers rehab instead of prison. I believe that we can deal with freedoms as long as we are educated and supported in it.

What is clear to me, Nir Eyal, and many others is that we have the power to upgrade our relationship with technology and live a more meaningful life by learning about tech's dark sides, upgrading our mindsets, and adjusting our digital usage patterns.

What Does Being Untethered Entail?

Before we dive any deeper I want to share my first secret to digital well-being with you.

Here it comes: Our smartphones are not just tools. In reality they are partners in one of our primary relationships. Hear me out on this one. I believe that we might just be in our first relationship with a digital device. One that looks nothing like a person or a robot but is by our side for longer than even our closest humans.

For most of my life I saw my smartphone as just a tool. I treated it like I would treat a pair of scissors, a knife, or a pencil. I left it on my desk, dining table, or bedside, always in plain sight. I thought of it just like I did any other tool. I believed that I would use my phone only when I needed or wanted to. But something was different about it. While the time I spent using most tools either stayed steady over the years or even went down—I really don't use pencils that often anymore—the time I spent with my smartphone kept increasing year over year for the past decade. But weirdly I did not feel more productive or any happier while using it. It didn't bring me more joy, and more frequently it felt like it took some away from me.

Imagine a chef or a passionate cook. When they spend more hours using knives and pans they produce more delicious food and often using those tools brings them joy too. But my smartphone kept creeping into my life even when I didn't want to be using it or didn't desire to have it close. I kept using it more often regardless of how it truly made me feel.

There lies the main difference between our smartphone and most other tools.

So, in my mind, I started placing my phone into a different category altogether. Instead of a tool, I started thinking of it as my first relationship with technology, my first relationship outside the human realm. In the beginning it was just an experiment. It felt silly. I thought it might even be a foolish way of looking at it. But I was committed to exploring what that would mean. I started learning about relationships, what makes them work or fail, I learned about codependency, toxicity, and boundary setting. The deeper I dove the cleared it became to me that many of those tools and thinking patterns apply to the context of our smartphone.

Whether naturally or through therapy, most of us learn over time how to have healthy relationships with our parents, siblings, wider family, friendships, colleagues, acquaintances and even our romantic partners (although not always at first try). What truly encourages me is that I have seen many of us start developing healthier relationships with our smartphones over the past few years. Every time I ask somebody about their phone usage they give me tips just like a couple would when asked about how to create a healthy romantic relationship.

How would you think about setting boundaries, or alone time if you thought of your device as a partner in your life? How would you make sure to get alone time when needed and show up for that relationship as your best version when you can?

Living an untethered life does not mean that we have to disconnect from our devices. Rather imagine it as moving in with our smartphone and establishing a healthy co-living relationship. You are still able to hang out with other people without bringing/using your phone. An untethered person is someone who embraces the relationship with their smartphones instead of replacing it with a dumbphone and hoping for the best. This one mindset shift enabled the start of a journey towards a healthy relationship with my devices and the untethered life I live today.

Our smartphones are amazing. You are amazing. Just as two great people can have a bad relationship with each other, so can we have an unhealthy relationship with our smart devices—and even ourselves. *Untethered* is all about supporting you in moving away from a toxic and codependent relationship with your smartphone to an untethered one. This book will help you redefine your routines, develop healthier digital habits, and live a more fulfilled life in control of your attention.

In this book, I won't advocate replacing your smartphone with a dumbphone. I am not even necessarily recommending that you reduce your technology use. Obviously, using your phone less can be part of the solution, but I don't think that reducing time spent with tech is the only answer. The answer comes from how we engage and relate with the digital world, how we treat ourselves, and what priority we give to our own digital well-being.

My goal is simply to help you become less tethered to your smartphone, to spend time with it more consciously, and to become more alive and focused on your purpose—with mobile devices as part of your journey.

This book is about upgrading your mind, creating new habits, and utilizing old ones to live a fulfilled life untethered from but in a healthy relationship with your tech devices, and especially your smartphone.

* * *

I began my own unhealthy relationship with technology over twenty years ago. I loved internet-enabled tech from the moment I had access to it. I built my own PCs, I was an elite player of online games such as Starcraft II and Diablo II, I spent $3,000 on a tablet to take notes with a pencil at school in 2004, and I even flew to the US from Europe to buy the first-generation Kindle. That's how much I loved technology.

This passion for tech manifested in my professional life as well. I spent years working on electric cars in Germany for BMW and then later at Lucid Motors in Silicon Valley. During my MBA at Berkeley, I focused on technology management and entrepreneurship. Later in my professional career, I worked for the company that invented the smartphone. At Apple's Cupertino headquarters, I was responsible for managing new product introductions, a dream role for somebody with my affinity for new tech.

But the years at Apple turned from living out my childhood dream to making me aware of just how powerful smartphones and other tech products truly are. I realized for the first time how broken our relationship with our smartphones is. I loved their endless potential, but I saw how every potential has a downside. For a while, I thought my smartphone overdependence—which you'll learn more about shortly—didn't impact my well-being because I was doing so well in life otherwise. I couldn't have been more wrong.

Indeed, my digital devices never prevented me from achieving professional milestones. I was a refugee as a child in 1992, and today I'm financially comfortable and living in Silicon Valley. But it did often hinder me from living a fulfilled life on my own terms. It took me until my early thirties to see how I was misusing tech as an excuse to live a shadow life instead of one I was truly satisfied with, not just one other people told me was great. A friend of mine with a similar affinity to his smartphone once said about himself that he was a "high functioning addict, able to achieve great milestones in life but always unhappy and out of control in his personal life." I could relate.

But I believe that the way I use my smartphone now makes me more human by giving me back time to connect with other humans—and even facilitating those connections. I had to understand how my brain was wired and how tech was influencing me, then learn and adopt new tools that helped me deal with the consequences of the attention economy.[11] Thanks to my experiences working at elite tech companies, years spent struggling with tech overuse, and what I've gleaned from interviewing industry experts and becoming a certified Digital Wellness Educator, I felt equipped to write this book to share what I've learned about developing a healthy relationship with my smartphone, with tech in general, and with myself.

I first tried solving the problem of smartphone dependency by changing external factors. I quit my job at Apple, temporarily moved from a large house into a van, and went on a silent meditation retreat. And even after all of that I still felt tethered to my smartphone. The changes I was seeking required me to first accept that I had an intimate relationship with my smartphone that had turned toxic along the way. Only then I was able to see solutions that would enable me to live life on my own terms rather than a life dictated by my distractions and habitual smartphone use.

I know now that until we find a way out of the attention-seeking trap presented through digital technologies, we will struggle to engage with the present moment and create the life we want. But I want you to know that there is hope. I believe that we each carry the power to walk our own path and use technology to help us along it, rather than holding us back..and maybe even help us become more human.

As a teen, I would disengage from life by watching lots of TV and playing online games. I felt hypnotized. It was the same hypnotic state I would experience years later when watching one YouTube video after another: absent, checked out, like my entire being was being pushed down a hole, downgraded by the constant distraction. And when we are in these hooked states during which time just seems to fly by, we live moment to moment without being present for any given one. My problem was never a lack of awareness of what was going on—it was missing the knowledge and willpower to correct my behaviors.

Unfortunately, it was only after giving up on my job and many possessions and losing a significant amount of money that I realized I had to take responsibility for my digital wellness and my future self. One that I could be proud of.

I wrote *Untethered* so that you too can become your fullest self and have a healthier relationship with your smartphone before it grabs hold of you the way it did with me. This book includes the knowledge, mindset changes, and tools you will need to start on this path and—most importantly—stick to it.

Now, you might be wondering exactly what technology did to me—or, should I say, what I did to myself with the help of technology. Before I could develop a healthy relationship with myself and my smartphone, my tech misuse would cost me some of my life savings—and at one point, nearly my life itself...

MY KRYPTONITE

My struggles with extensive tech use go way back to the late nineties, when I was eleven or twelve. Gaming, specifically playing multiplayer online games, was my favorite hobby and way of interacting with the world. Other nerds and online gaming geeks like me were my closest friends. It wasn't until one day in the summer of 2004, in my last year as a teen, that I became aware of how bad it had gotten when I arrived home after going on seventy-two hours without sleep.

I'd locked myself in my friend's basement for three days with six other guys who loved gaming. Most of us didn't sleep at all, myself included. I will never forget the image of my friend Danny, so tired that he fell asleep next to his open PC tower. His computer was overheating, so he had to increase airflow by opening the case of his tower, but I don't think he'd planned to rest his head in front of it.

I didn't realize it back then, but online multiplayer games would be my kryptonite for the rest of my life.

Needless to say, after seventy-two hours of gaming, I was exhausted. Arriving at home, my shaky hands grabbed the keys and slowly opened the door in the hope that nobody would see me in this state. I was looking pale, feeling exhausted, and my eyes were closing every couple of seconds. I didn't feel like talking to my family, so I sprinted to my room and locked the door. My body was a brick, my mouth was dry, and my mind felt like it had been hooked to a washing machine, endlessly spinning from exhaustion. I also felt ashamed.

I remember waking up fifteen hours later, feeling a little heavy and drowsy but much better than I could have imagined after gaming for seventy-two hours. (I still wish I had the physical recovery speed of my teenage years.) After regaining consciousness, I walked into the bathroom to wash my face with cold water. The cold water felt energizing, like a solar panel that had been suddenly hit by sunlight. My brain woke up and instantly started processing what had happened.

Wait. What had actually happened? While I seemed to remember with some clarity what had happened a couple of days earlier, I had a hard time tapping into the experience of the last few hours before falling asleep at home. Those memories seemed blurry, probably because my memory function had stopped working properly due of the lack of sleep. I was especially worried about the fact that I wasn't sure how I made it back home. Did I ride my moped? Did I crash? Did I get hurt? I honestly wasn't sure.

I spat out my toothpaste, rinsed my mouth with water, and rushed to take off all my clothes. I started looking at myself in the mirror, left and right, up and down. Surprisingly, not a single dent... but gosh was I pale! I was so happy to see that my body was okay. I felt more confident that everything was fine, so I put my clothes back on and stepped outside the bathroom to say hi to my family and have breakfast with them.

I was alive! And it seemed like I was being fed soon!

But as soon as I shut the bathroom door, I had a flashback. I remembered how I'd made it back home! I was standing in front of my moped, carrying a huge duffel bag with my computer tower in it. I was putting on my helmet. But my eyes were closing every few seconds out of exhaustion and because seeing the sun after seventy-two hours was too bright. But, being a teenager, I was still confident enough to step on my scooter and attempt to drive home. I mumbled a pact with myself: "You will not fall asleep on this drive! You will not crash!"

And then I took off.

But just a couple of minutes into the drive, my eyes started falling shut every few seconds again. I tried not to fall asleep with every bit of energy I had, as I had promised myself. I recalled the pact I'd made, but amended it slightly: "I promise to not fall asleep while riding my scooter, and in exchange I will give my eyes some rest by closing them every four seconds for one second."

It was a bad deal, but I needed to make one quickly before it was too late. So for the rest of my thirty-minute trip back home, I counted to four and closed my eyelids for a second before restarting the count. It wasn't a good idea, but it likely saved me.

I wondered what would have happened if the police had stopped me. Can you get arrested for being exhausted while driving? Ticketed for driving under the influence of computer games? I wasn't drunk; I hadn't done drugs. But I was still impaired. I was driving poorly, swerving in my lane, going way too slowly, and being honked at frequently—and worst of all, I had my eyes closed for 20 percent of the trip.

The flashback ended with my mum asking me if I'd enjoyed the long weekend.

"Did you guys end up playing your favorite computer games? I hope you got some sleep there, and I still can't believe you drove yourself and your computer equipment back home on your moped after being there for seventy-two hours," she said as if she had just experienced my flashback, too. I didn't want her to worry, so I lied and said that I'd slept well and that the drive had been no problem. Then I rushed to the kitchen to have breakfast.

As I crushed scrambled eggs and pork sausages, I wondered if I'd just been lucky or if it was the pact with myself that had saved me. I could have died driving myself home just because I hadn't wanted my parents to pick me up and see me in that state. My obsession with my computer and multiplayer games could have killed me. Plus, I had lied to my mum, and I hated myself for that.

It was the first time that I got a glimpse of the damaging effects gaming and technology could have on my life. Unfortunately, it wouldn't be the last time my obsession with digital tech would throw my life into disarray.

How I Lost $100K Glued to My Smartphone

While the seventy-two-hour gaming incident made clear my obsession with multiplayer games, I hadn't learned my lesson. I was a teenager, and I felt invincible. I continued to game and overuse my tech devices. It took me many more years to realize that I needed to stop gaming—more on how that happened later. But once I did, my promise to myself to avoid online games lasted for nearly ten years, before I got hooked on tech again and lost my life savings.

In September 1998, I was living in Innsbruck, Austria, a charming city in the middle of the Alps. From the center of the town, it was a fifteen-minute bus ride to the closest ski slope. The most important parts of the city were reachable by bike or foot. The center of the town was a no-driving zone and thus safe for kids to be around. We had hardly any criminal issues and only one homeless person that I knew of. The city had several parks, theaters, and sports centers.

But none of this mattered to me once I discovered computer games.

I was about to turn thirteen, and was hanging out at my friend Simon's house. My parents were chatting with his parents, so Simon and I were left to our own devices. He decided to show me a new game he'd got called Starcraft.

I got into it immediately. The game, set in the beginning of the twenty-sixth century, centers on a galactic struggle for domination between three distinct races—Zerg, Protoss, and Terran—that are perfectly balanced against each other in the fight for territorial ownership. And I wasn't alone—Starcraft eventually became the benchmark real-time-strategy game of its time, with a massive global following.

It was on that day that computer games slowly began to take over my life. Before computers and online gaming, I was an excellent student who enjoyed the nature surrounding Innsbruck. But around ninth grade, I began retreating from school to spend more time in virtual realms. It started with Starcraft, then Diablo 2, and later transformed into a love for shooter games like Medal of Honor. I was even recruited by several clans (the gaming equivalent of sports clubs) and often ended up on global leaderboards of the top one hundred players. The success made me feel like I was doing something right.

By eleventh grade, I was no longer interested in school. My life evolved around playing games and sometimes sports. It was all about competitive play. I was in a habitual state of competition against others and myself. I felt stressed out and irritable most of the time. But because I was good at games and winning often, I felt it was a price worth paying. Isn't being a winner and exceptional what society wants most for our boys?

While I did great in the online world, school was a different story. I knew that some of the most successful entrepreneurs were dropouts, so I didn't really mind that my grades were suffering. But in eleventh grade, my teachers told me that they weren't sure if I was good enough to progress to twelfth grade. They wanted me to repeat the year. In the last few weeks, I scrambled to find opportunities to show them that I was good enough. The thought of staying in school for longer than necessary frightened me just enough to put in the little extra effort needed to stay on track.

* * *

What happened to me is in no way unusual. Once games went from being fun single-player exercises to social competitions on a global scale, kids started spending many more hours online. The marriage of social validation with dopamine rewards has created generations of hooked gamers. I was part of the first generation that was introduced to the concept of multiplayer online games and their addictive potential.

I didn't fully realize how limited my life had become until I moved in with roommates for the first time. I was playing so much that I hardly spent any time with them. I still remember the moment when one of them made me aware of my video game addiction.

We were at home, I was playing, and they were watching a movie together. They invited me to join them multiple times, but I wanted to keep playing. At some point our internet connection went down, and my hero in the game froze. A few seconds later the internet was back up, but my hero had been killed.

I flipped out on my roommates. The anger I felt in that moment was so deep, so fiery, that I couldn't have held it back. All the stress that had built playing games suddenly came bursting out.

After my outburst, my roommate Ivan, one of the kindest people you could ever meet, said, "Dude, it's just a game. Let's connect, have a drink, and watch the movie together." I didn't join them—I was still too angry. But it struck me like lightning: What the hell am I doing with my life? What was the purpose of this life spent playing online games? I wasn't even truly enjoying the experience.

That was the moment I decided to make a big change. I uninstalled all my games, and stopped playing for nearly ten years ...

... But even after that many years, I still was deeply hooked to my devices. I was consuming online content for hours every day and I didn't need actual games to keep me engaged, since most apps seemed to have incorporated some level of gamification and social interaction. But my overuse of my smartphone in particular did not become obvious until online games came back into my life.

A couple of years ago, a good friend invited me to play a mobile game with him. Normally, I would have said no, but I thought, How bad could it be to play a little with a friend? I should have known myself better…I didn't have a standalone computer anymore but our smartphones are now more powerful than PCs in the nineties were—more powerful and always conveniently available, just waiting to be picked out of our pockets.

The first day, I played for an hour with my friend. The next day, I played without him for about two hours. By the end of the month, I was up to eight hours per day. I couldn't resist the game. I cancelled most of my other plans so I could play all day. It seemed like I wanted to catch up on years of not playing in a month. I also felt like games had become more engaging since I'd stopped playing.

The past decade hadn't necessarily led to better games or in-game experiences. Rather, developers seemed to have focused their attention on developing the most engaging games possible, games you couldn't resist spending many hours on. That was a major problem for me, and I assume for many other gamers too.

During the few weeks I was playing online games again, I felt unfulfilled, empty, and out of control of my own life. I started to feel sadness and a mild depression creeping in. I couldn't keep a schedule, I constantly made excuses for why I wasn't able to make progress on projects, and my sleep schedule was all over the place. It became clear that I had to recommit myself to a life without online games. I promised I wouldn't touch them again if I wasn't able to have a healthy relationship with them—not because I didn't enjoy them when I played them casually, but because I am unable to limit myself to casually playing games. I easily get hooked to the feeling of flow and excitement that online games provide.

I needed the excitement, the dopamine rush, and even the disappointment associated with gaming. Studies have shown that I am not alone in desiring achievement, escape, and immersion.[12] About half of Americans play video games and share similar desires for doing so.

Although I had mentally decided to give up games, my body had gotten used to the dopamine rush it experienced while gaming. So I soon found another way to replicate this excitement outside of the gaming world.

I started watching tons of video content on YouTube and tried to distract myself with social media, but it just didn't provide the rush my subconscious mind and body desired. But with the stock market all over the news and people reportedly making tons of money, I thought about investing my money as well. I subscribed to several YouTube channels and thought I was learning by getting "expert" investing advice.

These YouTubers shared their investing know-how and their favorite platforms to invest on, and they made it seem so easy. "You too could make a million bucks!" they would regularly shout. So I opened a trading account on Robinhood and started investing on my smartphone. Investing soon just felt like another game—but one with even bigger real-life consequences.

Although I had studied behavioral economics with a focus on finance and investing, I did not expect that even trading platforms had become gamified over the years. Maybe because their developers share the same incentive structure, to keep you on their respective platforms for as long as possible. The more time you spend, the more likely you are to spend more money with them...

I started getting hooked on Robinhood similarly to how I had online games. I got into day trading, the most exciting and stressful way of playing the stock market, and soon discovered that it provided me with the same rush gaming did. After a while, I was gambling with bigger and bigger amounts...

Some trading days were great, and I was able to make thousands of dollars. One day, I made $45,000! Insane! My risk appetite rose, and I thought I could make a living doing this—until it went bad, quickly. First it was $10,000, then $20,000 in losses. I started to fear not being able to make it all back. But I was hooked by all of the app's game-like experiences. I wasn't making rational decisions. I was playing a game. And I didn't stop until I'd gambled away a significant chunk of my life savings—$100,000.

* * *

I don't know what your digital kryptonite is, or if you even have one. What I do know is that the average American spends close to twelve and a half hours connected to media through tech devices—every single day! That is more than I spent playing games in my peak weeks!

Whether you struggle to put down your phone because of YouTube, TikTok, or Netflix, or you spend hours endlessly scrolling social media sites like Facebook, Twitter, or Snapchat, or you obsessively follow your favorite celebrity/influencer on Twitch, Clubhouse, or Instagram, it doesn't really matter. Most of us have experienced the defeated feeling of being stuck in an endless tech loop through one app or another.

I was shocked by how quickly my obsession with gamified systems had turned into gambling—and that it could even happen in the first place! I had to realize how powerful my smartphone truly was when I was not in control. I had never lost that much money before. It was depressing, and it turned my entire life upside down. For example, I had to delay buying a house I really wanted. The experience taught me that I needed to find ways to develop a healthy relationship with the devices in my life or I could lose the rest of my money…or even worse, my life.

After all, people have died in front of their computers from neglecting their physical, mental, and emotional needs.[13] Over- or misuse of technology negatively impacts our emotional processing capabilities, our attention, and our decision-making abilities. Studies link anxiety, depression, and a rise in suicide attempts to the use of smartphones, tablets and other devices. The struggle is real for most of us, some more and some less. I believe that it is time for us to develop a healthier and untethered relationship with our devices!

If after reading my story you are still unsure whether many of us have a toxic relationship with our devices, let me show you some data from arguably the most affected in society. Children might be the most negatively influenced by our lack of knowledge and education around appropriate smartphone use.

Ontario, Canada's Centre for Addiction and Mental Health conducts a health survey every two years in grades seven through twelve.[14] The most recent survey was pre-COVID, in 2019, and showed the following changes between 2017 and the time of the survey. The number of kids reporting fair or poor physical health went up by about 24 percent, fair or poor mental health by 41 percent, low self-esteem by 41.5 percent, serious psychological distress by 20.5 percent, and suicidal ideation by 20.5 percent. Seven out of ten kids also reported three or more hours of screen time daily, up by 18.5 percent, and five or more hours on electronic devices daily in free time, a 20 percent increase.

Sure, this might just all be correlation and not causation. But is that likely? It seems to me that if we continue using our devices throughout the next decade in the same ways we have been in the past, that these alarming numbers will only increase, and by then it might be too late to reverse the trend.

The strategies I learned and developed as a result of my relapse helped me create a more purposeful, ritual-driven life, one free from tech dependence. The money is gone, but I have my health and passion for life back. I honestly feel more human than ever before, now that I have developed an untethered relationship with my smartphone. But most importantly, the biggest financial loss of my life motivated me to help others manage their relationship with tech—and led me to write the book you're reading right now.

UNTETHERED: A GUIDE TO CREATING A HEALTHY RELATIONSHIP WITH DIGITAL TECHNOLOGIES

"Screentime isn't necessarily an accurate gauge for whether some-one is using their favorite platforms problematically."

- **Mark Griffith**, internet use researcher at Nottingham Trent University[15]

Our smartphones are not inherently bad. Yes, they are extremely powerful—more powerful than anything else we consume regularly, but not bad or harmful by themselves.

And for most people, neither is alcohol. It would be irresponsible not to acknowledge that for some people, even a small amount of alcohol is unmanageable. Globally, alcohol misuse is the seventh highest risk factor for premature death or disability.[16] Alcoholism is a real addiction for many, and it should be treated seriously. Thus, the comparison with our smartphone usage might not be perfect.

That said, my life without smartphones or alcohol—even though I only drink socially every other week—would have been less rich and interesting. However, I've also experienced periods in my life where I've misused each of them. While finding the right balance for alcohol consumption is simply a part of growing up for most of us, it doesn't seem to work that way for how we use technology. As a society, we seem to lack agreement on what constitutes technology misuse—or that it even exists.

Being untethered means being able to disconnect from our devices and enjoy the beauty of life without needing our smartphones around all the time. Being untethered means being in control of our well-being, rather than allowing our smartphones to dictate it. It does not mean, however, giving up on technology. Our goal with untethering is to develop a set of strategies and tools that help us find fulfillment without ditching all of our devices.

Don't get me wrong—this book won't keep you from unconsciously scrolling or overplaying games ever again. Rather, the tools and techniques in here will help you develop a healthy relationship with your smartphone and become more conscious about your tech use. The alternative is what we have right now: most Americans fill any void in their life by tapping on their smartphones. As of 2020, about 88 percent of Americans feel uneasy leaving their phone at home.[17] Because it affects the majority of us, this phenomenon has received its own name: nomophobia ("no mobile phone phobia").

Isn't it strange that I have to highlight the ability to leave your house without your smartphone as something special? Being untethered means being able to go for a walk without bringing your phone and still feeling complete.

Untethered will give you the knowledge, mindset changes, and tools that will support you on a path to developing a healthy relationship with yourself and your devices. I will show how your smartphone and the apps on it can captivate you, how you can "upgrade" your mind to move away from this dependency, and the concrete tools that will help you gain control over your habitual smartphone usage, live a more fulfilled life, and most importantly, create a better relationship with yourself. In the chapters that follow you will learn how to become a more alive version of yourself even in these times of constant distraction.

We'll start by exploring how our tech distracts us; this understanding will form a basis to help you deal with distractions for the rest of your life. In the next chapter, we will examine five external trends that contribute to our unhealthy relationship with ourselves and our digital devices. As our world becomes increasingly more complex, our understanding of what is real is being challenged. Because of the proliferation of fake news, artificially created photos and videos and alternative belief systems, it has become easier than ever to guide us astray, misinform us, and use our brains against us to capture our most valuable currency—our attention.

Understanding these external trends is just the beginning. In part II of the book, we'll dive deeper into mindset, exploring how our thinking patterns and internal programming can contribute to an unhealthy relationship with tech. We will explore four mindset shifts or upgrades that will enable us to create and walk a path of minimal distraction and maximum happiness.

I am convinced that in the future, a happy life will be less defined by the simple goals of prior generations. Living a good life will depend less on metrics like money, power, marriage, kids, and status. It is more likely to depend on having a healthy relationship with oneself, other people, and our devices. Those relationships will define the inputs we feed ourselves. More than just the food we eat, it will be the type of information we consume that feeds our satisfaction with life. What we put into our physical body, mind and soul is what defines us and our capability to be happy, peaceful and fulfilled. Part II will give you the knowledge you need to upgrade your mind and create a healthier relationship with yourself and the tech in your life.

And finally, in part III, we will discuss a set of tools that can be used every day to create and maintain a healthy relationship with your smartphone. I won't recommend that you stop using your smartphone altogether—or even use it significantly less. But I will give you tools to calm your mind, see your actions for what they are, and cultivate a life that doesn't require you to be glued to your smartphone. These tools will help you regain control over your tech.

A word of advice: You might feel the urge to skip parts I and II and jump into the "meat" of the book. I understand that it may be tempting to look for the quickest solutions, but I ask you to resist this urge because you will miss some core insights. In a way, jumping right to those quick fixes is like taking antidepressants. Sometimes they are urgently needed. If that is you, professional help might be better than reading *Untethered*. But antidepressants are not the best long-term solution for most of us. I recommend you first attempt to understand the trends causing our tech misuse and the mindset changes that are necessary for building a better relationship.

We are going through change on a global, societal and individual level, and it's coming full steam ahead. I like to think of the coronavirus outbreak as just a starting point to massive changes within and outside of ourselves. To thrive in the new world, you will have to deeply understand yourself and the socioeconomic milieu in which you find yourself. Instead of simply downloading information from the internet, or scrolling through social media, you need to become fully aware of the important changes we are seeing now—because they are giving us an opportunity to upgrade our lives.

Instead of being downgraded by the systems around you, you can ignite a new light within you and break free from feeling hooked—a truly untethered life! And, understand that nobody else will do this for you. You are fully responsible for your destiny. Luckily, you carry the power to do it within yourself. I trust in you, and I hope that this book will help you discover the forces affecting your relationship with tech, allow you to overcome mobile distractions, recognize some truths you already hold within yourself, and take the first steps on your path toward an untethered life.

The External Trends
Affecting Our Tech Usage

I started writing this book just before the first wave of quarantines hit Oakland, California, during the 2020 coronavirus outbreak. Many people were afraid of physical contact with others. We developed new social greeting norms, new ways of living in a contactless world. Many of Silicon Valley's tech startups decided to introduce a mandatory work-from-home policy to prevent the virus from spreading among their workforce.

During the outbreak, most of us spent less time in public places. Businesses that included physical space as their core offering suffered. Friends in the hotel industry reported that hotels that typically ran at 90 percent occupancy were down to 20 percent by mid-2020. A restaurant owner told me that his business changed from a place to eat good food to a delivery hub fulfilling online orders. He had reduced his workforce in the kitchen and hired people who could help manage the flow of incoming online orders. Conferences, festivals, and other large gatherings were canceled outright or experienced a significant drop in attendance.

I am sure many books will be written about the virus outbreak. It pushed our physical and mental limits and turned us into home-bound hermits with all the consequences thereof. We likely have never been this close to some of our friends and family while being physically distant from most of society. Just think about it: how many new people entered your life this year compared to prior ones?

Regardless of your individual experience through this disaster, one thing almost all of us have shared is an increase in screen time. All corners of the internet exploded during COVID. Our online use went up so much that we were literally breaking the internet's capabilities! Between Q2 2019 and Q2 2020, the amount of streamed content increased by almost 75 percent, forcing European network providers to ask Netflix to reduce the streaming quality of their videos. And the number of subscriptions we used increased as well. Every fourth American increased their number of streaming services, according to Nielsen's August 2020 Total Audience Report.[18]

Beyond the traditional players, we saw new apps receiving lots of attention. It seems that we want to do more than just connect through messaging and text. We want to hear, see, and experience each other. Apps like Zoom, Duo, and Houseparty allow groups to join a single video chat to talk, dance or play games together. Houseparty saw their user base grow by about 80 percent between the end of January 2020 and March 2020 alone.

Obviously, this is not news to anybody. After all, we had more time and we couldn't really go outside of our homes for much of 2020! But the iPhone has already been around for thirteen years and changed how we access and consume digital information even before the virus outbreak. It only forced us to embrace the potential of the digital world more deeply. We are already and will be even more so shaped by digital information in the future. Instead of experiencing the physical world directly, we will continue to consume information and create our own reality through second-hand experiences over the internet.

And while I am more excited for the future than ever before, there are scary sides to moving more of our lives online. A large percentage of what we know is and will no longer be shaped by our experience of the physical world. How will we be sure of what is true when information can be generated and shared digitally without being rooted in reality?

In the physical world, the rules are well defined and clearly understood. We rely on the laws of physics to understand why and how the world functions, and we have millions of years of gene pool development to help us intuitively and emotionally understand the world around us. Our intuitive responses have been shaped to perfection by our environment over millennia. They prevent us from getting too close to an open fire, help us decide whether or not to eat an unfamiliar piece of fruit, and even guide us in selecting a partner through visual and scent preferences.

These tools that are given to us at birth and that we develop throughout our lives are tremendously useful and simultaneously underutilized. We've already been given very sharp knives, but most of us don't use these knives, this inner knowing, extensively. Often, it is not even accessible to us, covered by expectations, hurts and life experiences that lead us astray. But in times where reality can be created in Photoshop, this inner guidance might even mislead us. In the digital world, we have a harder time understanding what is real, while chambers of alternative truths are becoming easier to access.

We could be entering a post-truth era where fake news and alternative beliefs such as flat earth theory are becoming more popular because of how easy they spread online. At some moments, such as during peak election cycles, people actually share more fake news than actual news on platforms like Facebook, which just incentivizes content creators to create more fake news.[19]

It shouldn't come as a surprise that the most tech-savvy generations—millennials and Gen Zers—are the most likely to believe in "alternative" theories. Among eighteen- to twenty-four-year-old Americans, only two thirds have a firm belief in a round globe.[20] While in the past it would have been hard to build community around alternative beliefs, it is now easy to find like-minded people online. And because it is so easy to share knowledge, we can also find "proofing evidence" for every alternative belief held.

The digital world is new to us. We're built to live in small communities where we know and trust everybody. We're born with instincts that often help us in real life but fail us online. Zoom fatigue shows how our ability to read people's gestures helps us understand them in the real world, but trying to do the same thing on a 2D screen while looking at twenty-five faces simultaneously overwhelms us. But the average American now spends most of their waking hours digitally connected. It's become our de facto real world, and sometimes I wonder if we're even close to cut out for it.

The online world is not only overwhelming, it's also used too often as an escape from our lives and problems. In that way, it's similar to alcohol. Binge watching or binge drinking are just two ways to avoid dealing with ourselves and our problems. A 2015 study of binge watchers found significant escapism when compared to viewers who were deliberately planning to watch shows.[21] Binge watchers were significantly more likely to admit to watching to "pass time" and "forget life for a while."

In her 2016 thesis, "Pricking The Monster: Netflix and the modification of how and what we watch," Lauren Greene makes a similar claim: "The vast majority of people don't watch movies because they are culturally relevant or critically acclaimed, but because they want to escape certain realities."[22] We've done it with TV for years, but isn't it so much more convenient when a service like Netflix offers us instant availability based on our preferences, right on our smartphone!? Isn't it easier to open a mobile game app and engage in mindless screen time that way?

We are being buttered up while the world is rapidly becoming more digital and more complex, and it's challenging our ability to cope. Information overload, zoom fatigue, phubbing,[23] doomscrolling,[24] endless gamification, fear of surveillance, and the always-on culture are just some of the negative consequences of the attention economy. These factors are pushing us to rethink how we design a way of life that promotes optimal health and well-being, one in which our smartphones are integrated into our lives and allow us to live more fully in our in-person and digital communities, and in closer alignment with nature.

In the next few chapters, we will explore five major trends that are causing our overdependence on digital technologies. I believe that it is crucial to start by understanding the major external forces that shape our own behaviors before we can improve our digital well-being! We are bombarded by online attractions, distractions, and pleasures every day. It's time to take a step back and bring awareness to the trends driving them.

Let's dive into these distractions and attractions and learn how the digital world captures our attention so easily. I want to spend the next chapters presenting the top five external factors that are overwhelming to our human design and the effects they have on us, amplified by internet-enabled technologies.

TREND #1: INCREASING COMPLEXITY

The world is an extraordinarily complex place. When our smartphones stop turning on one day out of nowhere, most of us don't know how to fix it. Other than holding and releasing a button or or two in the hope that the machine's failures will resolve themselves, we're pretty much hopeless.

The same is probably true when your car breaks down and you have to take it to a mechanic. Or when your home internet goes down and you have to call your provider to fix it. In general, when any of the things you take for granted fail to work properly, what's revealed to you is complexity itself.

Our lives are supported by complex machines that we don't fully understand. It's impossible to know everything. But at some point, all human beings had very similar levels of knowledge, much like animals might today. We all knew how to find food and water, and how to build a shelter. We knew how to survive in alignment with Mother Nature.

Complexity has enabled us to move away from that way of living, but we're also less in tune with basic survival skills. Most people understand what it takes to survive in society today but can't grow food or identify edible vs. poisonous plants. Complexity drives us to let go of some knowledge in order to deepen it in other areas. Because there is so much to know, we can only focus on certain topics.

Complexity is also not a constant, but rather increases over time. Just forty years ago, there was no personal computer or smartphone. Public availability of the internet was more than a decade away. How did we share pictures or stay connected with our families, you might ask? How did I find cat videos to adore? Well, there were solutions. Just simpler, more expensive, less convenient ones.

People wrote mail or used their expensive house phones to stay connected, and when they wanted to exchange pictures they got them developed in a physical photo shop and mailed copies to their relatives. AT&T was the only telephone operator in the US. No competition meant it was extremely expensive by today's standards. Also, about half of the human population (2.2 billion people) was cut off from the rest of humanity due to being poor or living under repressive regimes.

Just forty years ago, we were so isolated from each other that finding a date meant approaching a stranger in real life, either at a bar or through friends or family, instead of connecting on a dating app with one click. (Roughly 40 percent of couples met online in 2019, compared to about 20 percent in 2010, and just over 5 percent in 2000.)[25] How inconvenient that must have been!

Forty years ago was also when my parents were in their twenties, meaning they were adults and had kids before the internet was available. They were my age before they had access to the internet. It blows my mind to think about it.

Since then, a wide range of technologies has significantly changed our social environment. The digitization of a vast majority of information has decreased living costs and increased humanity's collective wealth. Today, most of us are connected with one another on social media; we tell the world what it's like to work at our companies on Glassdoor and rate businesses on Yelp. We share our thoughts online and are often more truthful due to a sense of anonymity then we even are with friends and family.

The increased wealth, explosion of technologies, and our willingness to integrate them into our lives has made the world more connected and much more complex. Many of us have gone from consumers of media to active content creators on sites like Medium, Facebook, Instagram, TikTok, YouTube, and Wikipedia. We share information and knowledge with each other twenty-four hours a day. This creates not only diversity but depth of knowledge, out of which new information and technologies are created. More technologies, more engagement, and more information lead to more complexity.

And complex systems turn out to be unforgiving places for people and companies who move slowly or can't adapt to their environment. Complex systems require us to change with the flow of information, with the creation of new technologies and with the change of social rules and dynamics. This is not for everybody. Especially not for many people in the oldest age group (sixty-five and older) who have learned and succeeded doing things their way for most of their adult life. Many of them had one job their entire life.

Out of all of this, it is important to recognize one major fact: Complex systems are harder to control than simple systems. We spend our entire lives trying to control the complexities around us. Whether that means studying a subject at university, learning to manage our finances, or figuring out how to find and keep a romantic partner, learning is always also about being in more control. And as the complexity of the human world accelerates, so does our fear of not being able to control it.

But what exactly is "complexity?" The physics Nobel laureate Murray Gell-Mann once said that "a variety of different measures would be required to capture all our intuitive ideas about what is meant by complexity." And this time is probably no different. Complexity is a collection of features rather than a single phenomenon, so quantifying it with a single metric is difficult.[26] However, what we can do is define the characteristics of such features.

According to the University of Groningen, there are several key characteristics that most complex systems share:[27]

1. **Fundamental uncertainty and limited predictability**: Complex adaptive systems are extremely hard to predict in great detail.

2. **Self-organization**: Complex systems tend to operate without central control. They have order, but typically organize themselves from the bottom up.

3. **Nonlinearity, tipping points, and large events**: Relatively small changes can lead to large events. Complex systems show nonlinear dynamics and can move from a high degree of stability to unstable behavior quickly. Just think of what the iPhone did to non-smartphones or digital cameras, or how COVID-19 led to the destruction and creation of trillions in value.

4. **Emergence**: Higher-level behavior cannot simply be derived by aggregating behavior at the level of the elements. The whole is more than the sum of its parts. This higher order was typically not intended by the elements.

5. **Evolutionary dynamics**: Complex systems are characterized by a cycle of variation-selection-multiplication. The system is never at rest. There is no end point or equilibrium, only constant change and innovation.

Complex systems like our society, the economy, the human body, and our brains all share these same characteristics. Understanding them can help us imagine what our future might be like, assuming that complexity will continue to increase over time.

It scares me to think that in complex systems, we are bound to have less control over the results of our actions due to limited predictability and nonlinearity. As new technologies emerge and systems self-organize in novel ways constantly, we should expect to have more difficulty understanding the relationship between input and output!

In college and grad school, I learned how to strategize, make decisions, and manage risks to increase revenues or decrease costs. Making outcomes more predictable and controllable was the goal. But as the environment we live in becomes more complex, we have to start recognizing that our ability to control our external circumstances decreases.

Living in an unpredictable, self-organizing system has consequences on the human psyche. Self-organization refers to the process by which individuals organize through interactions amongst themselves. But the need to self-organize can reduce the sense of belonging for many of us as building that community now requires more effort and practice. The term "hard to predict" basically means that it's harder to feel ownership over one's future.

This shows up at every level of society. On a personal level, we see people feeling like they have fewer social connections as the effort required to maintain them has increased due to an ever increasing number of alternatives.[28] On a national level, we are seeing the powerlessness of our democracy in a world that has become too fast paced and complex for us to understand. It likely comes as no surprise that global uncertainty levels have risen significantly over the past decade. For example, the International Monetary Fund has been tracking uncertainty since the sixties through its World Uncertainty Index. Unsurprisingly, we experienced peak global uncertainty at the early stages of the Covid pandemic.[29]

Take the internet. It's one of humanity's biggest accomplishments, if not the biggest. It's being constantly shaped by billions of people with different interests. Each one of us can create the next big thing on it, whether it's the meme of the day or a product to cure cancer. We are all just little tiny data blinks in the World

Wide Web, but we are all individually creating this large system of information together. Even though the internet has no body of control, it is extremely complex and its future is unpredictable.

And governments around the world are scared by the web's power. Between 2010 and 2011, social media played a significant role in facilitating communication among participants of political protests during the Arab Spring (a series of anti-government protests, uprisings, and armed rebellions that spread across much of the Arab world). Protestors used social media to organize demonstrations and raise local and global awareness of what was happening. Meanwhile, some governments fear losing control over their people and grasp for more power by censoring access to the internet. In China and several other countries, political and social media access is highly restricted.[30]

And it makes sense why they would. Just think about how little control our government has on the internet: it's relatively easy to find illegal drugs on the internet, but much harder for the government to crack down on the sellers. Or take the rapid spread of "fake news" and other disinformation online in recent years. How can the government uphold its duty to ensure a democratic process, when it can't find and control the people who create disinformation in the first place?

Some politicians understand that central control is slowly disappearing. Others try to restore control by blaming and vilifying other people or organizations. It is easy to blame people for not doing what we want because the system itself has become so unpredictable.

As we have learned from the characteristics of complex systems above, small changes can lead to large events.

One example of this kind of unexpected side effect is the implementation of noncompete clauses on the state level. While I was working for BMW on their electric cars, I had a noncompete agreement, meaning I wasn't able to work for another car company for several months after leaving BMW.

But California doesn't allow for noncompete clauses between businesses and their employees. This little difference in how California does business compared to, say, Massachusetts, allowed Silicon Valley to emerge as a hub of innovation in California rather than somewhere else.[31] Did California lawmakers anticipate the large effect this decision would have? Maybe, but it's unlikely.

The state of California has even gone so far as to define that companies cannot prevent a former employee from taking a new job even if it is likely that they will use prior secrets to perform well in their new role. Instead, businesses must simply wait and see if there is a violation, then prove that the former employee misappropriated confidential information in their new role.

Unsurprisingly, businesses are constantly trying to fight this law. At the same time, it has allowed for more knowledge transfer across business borders. Think of it as an online marketplace for companies. California's no-noncompete law has made previously secret information more accessible to many, so that all of us can learn and grow from it.

Complexity Makes Us Smarter but Asks for Flexibility

Over the past few decades, we've developed god-like technologies and put them in the hands of billions of people. As Yuval Noah Harari eloquently describes it in Homo Deus: "The individual is becoming a tiny chip inside a large system that nobody really understands." Nobody fully understands how they fit into this large system, and frankly, it would be impossible to find out. But we continue to contribute to it, sharing information with each other every single day, making the system more complex.

I believe that the driving force for every complex technology we create, and for the general complexity we are contributing to, is a desire to connect more deeply with the world, to explore the nuances around us and within us. Complexity, rather than being evil, is the natural outcome of our inherent interest to explore. Exploration creates new, more complex environments and, consequently, more complex beings. It also makes us smarter.

In 1982, James Flynn discovered that every generation seems to be performing better on IQ tests than prior generations.[32] Part of the reason this is happening is because the world around us is getting more complex and demands higher intellectual capabilities to be understood.

On a personal level, I've had to come to terms with the fact that an increase in complexity also comes with some loss of control. As I understand less of the complex tech being introduced, I've struggled with feeling less in control, especially as somebody who's spent most of his career guiding outcomes for companies in program and product management roles.

This phenomenon shows up in the financial system, too. As it becomes harder to understand the technologies developed by corporations, it becomes more likely that we will use other measures to evaluate a company's performance. How else could Tesla have become the most valuable car manufacturer of all time, worth more than Ford and GM combined, while selling a mere 3 percent of their volume?

Elon Musk's brand value, and how he controls our attitude toward him and his work (through Twitter, for example) might have something to do with that. He is one of the most well-known people in the world and because of his following can literally bend financial markets to his will just by tweeting about things. For example, the price of dogecoin, a cryptocurrency that started as a joke, rose 50 percent in the beginning of 2021 after Elon Musk tweeted about it.[33] One 2019 financial market study confirms that, "Twitter sentiment changes are effective in predicting short term stock trends."

Complexity makes the external world less controllable, so we seek refuge in simpler ways of understanding the world such as blind faith in whatever Elon says. He is very smart and successful, so he must know. But the truth is that we are handing over control because the world is too elaborate for us to fully understand.

The main lesson here is that there will be more areas of this world that we will no longer understand as our systems become more complex. But—and this is important—just because we don't understand the inner workings of the blockchain, autonomous driving, or artificial intelligence does not mean that we don't have some control over our future.

We Want to Trust, but We Prefer Control

We can't know everything. Instead, we have to trust that others do, that they will make good decisions with their knowledge, and that they will handle difficult decisions with the same care and understanding we might. You have to trust in humanity when losing control. Trust is the gateway to our individual and collective futures. We will talk more about what trusting in your abilities might entail in part II.

Meanwhile, many of us have found an external way to regain confidence and the perception of control, and that's through our smartphones. We check the news every day, turn on notifications, and use calendars and productivity apps to parcel out our days, all so that we can feel some measure of control over our world. We believe that by knowing more about what is happening in the world we can somehow have more control.

Even on just a physical level, phones provide us with something familiar to hold onto—literally. They're a place we know well, where we feel safe. It's so comforting to be in the digital world we enter through our smartphones that about 34 percent of us walk down the street with a smartphone in our hand.[34] But when a man and a woman walk together, that number goes down to 18 percent.

There are many explanations for why people carry their phones in their hands when they're not using them. They include the desire to be instantly available, or wanting to simply show off. But I think that a bigger part of it is a psychological dependence and need for control. We get anxious when we're separated from our phones, because they provide us with a sense of power. We can quickly look up information, change the song we are listening to or see where on the map we are. Just holding our phones reminds us of the power and control they give us. In a world that's becoming more complex and information rich every day, it's natural for us to seek control wherever we can find it.

For example, in the past few years, humans around the world have elected leaders who've promised a sense of control by going back to the "old days." This is a way of at least feeling in charge in a world that feels like it's moving forward uncontrollably.

In similar ways, our need to be with our smartphones is growing, too. Smartphones represent a familiar environment that we know well and feel like we can control. Every year, we check our devices about 10 percent more often. But like the devil who can only make empty promises, so are our phones full of the promise of control that they can't truly satisfy because the content in them is controlled by others. But more about this in Influences #2 and #3.

A 2019 study of two thousand Americans by Asurion discovered that, on average, we check our phones ninety-six times per day, a 20 percent increase compared to a similar study Asurion conducted in 2017.[35]

Social media and news outlets also feed our desire for more control. They know we like to click on extreme news, so they make us believe the world is a negative and evil place, an uncontrollable environment.

The truth is, no matter what the media wants you to believe, the world is becoming a better place in many ways. We will talk about news, media, and the state of the world in the next chapter, but for now I want you to recognize one thing: complexity reduces our ability to control the world we live in, but it actually doesn't matter that much, because true control comes from within! It is normal to want to find control through our devices, but you don't need to hold onto your phone. As long as you have ownership over your body and mind, you can change your world. We'll discuss how to establish that ownership in depth in parts II and III.

Now that we've discussed the tremendous complexity that surrounds us, let's talk about how this complex world is being presented to us by the media and how things are in reality.

Key Takeaways

- Previous generations grew up in a significantly less complex or connected world.

- Complex systems are fundamentally uncertain, extremely hard to predict, continuously changing, operating without control, and highly interconnected.

- Complexity is the outcome of our inherent interest in exploring the world deeply. It is something to embrace, not fear.

- Checking the news, using calendars and productivity apps, and physically holding onto our phones all creates an illusion of control; true control comes from within.

Trend #2: Negative Media Bias

If you're paying attention to the news these days, you might conclude that the world is becoming a worse place. A variety of crises are reported on constantly, and even when there's no sign of a crisis, we can rely on negative commentary on the internet to make us feel miserable as a last resort.

The news has become more negative over the past several decades. And while it would be easy to blame newspapers for reporting more extreme points of view, they do so partly because we're so receptive to negative reporting.

Newspapers, like every company, want to survive. Traditional media outlets have been struggling for years as the digital world has been flooded with unpaid content. We have decided to cut our household spending on newspapers and watch YouTube or use news apps for free instead. And while older generations average around seven hours of TV consumption per day, Gen Z has cut that consumption to about a quarter. They're more likely to stay up to date by searching the internet and consuming video content online.

In order to draw in more customers, news outlets decided to go with what worked in the past: focusing on the extreme.

This is not just a felt experience; sentiment analysis of BBC articles confirms the move toward more captivating language.[36] Kalev Leetaru, cocreator of the Global Database of Events, Language and Tone, is one of the first people to discover that the choice of words in media has become more negative over the years.

This didn't happen from one moment to the next. News outlets adjusted to more negative sentiment slowly, with the real shift starting sometime in the late nineties. It should be no surprise that this was also when online news started playing a larger role in our lives.

According to Kalev's research, by the late nineties, around 15 percent of news was delivered online; a decade later it was close to half. To put it in his words, "The data suggests a fascinating possibility: that the plunge towards negativity of media across the entire world was due to the rise of the Web itself and the increased competition that news outlets now faced."

We have an inclination to pay attention to negative rather than positive information.[37] Research shows that a negative perspective is more contagious than a positive perspective. And it makes sense! For our cave-occupying ancestors, alertness to danger was truly a matter of life or death. "We inherited the genes that predispose us to give special attention to those negative aspects of our environments that could be harmful to us," explains psychologist and happiness researcher Timothy J. Bono, PhD, who teaches a course on the "science of happiness" at Washington University in St. Louis.

All this negativity in the news has real-world consequences. Media outlets' negative bias has actually changed how we perceive the world. People estimate the chances of an event actually happening by how easily it comes to mind. That works in many situations, except for when the information we hold is less positive than the true state of things. Because of the way the media has portrayed the world recently, we are now more likely to overestimate how bad the world around us actually is.[38] In the end, perception creates reality. And our perception is that human civilization, based on what news is telling us, is in much worse shape than it actually is.

A lot of young people I've spoken to have decided to stay away from news and politics completely. We all get tired of overly distorted negative news. We get desensitized. We sometimes even start questioning whether we can be safe outside our own houses. We stop trusting others. We believe civilization is about to collapse. And the more we see life through overly negative lenses, the greater the likelihood we will fail, that we won't be able to recover from the next crisis or solve the next major global threat.

The negativity the media has been communicating to us affects how we communicate over the internet as well. Expressions of positive affect (positive emotions and expression, including cheerfulness, pride, enthusiasm, energy, and joy) are more or less stagnating worldwide, while negative affect (negative emotions and expression, including sadness, disgust, lethargy, fear, and distress) is on the rise. Simply put, we're expressing ourselves more negatively, a direct consequence of the media reporting a more negative picture of the world.

GLOBAL HAPPINESS OVER TIME

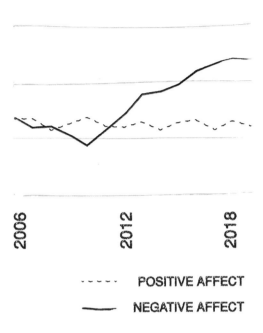

2006   2012   2018

- - - - -   POSITIVE AFFECT

———   NEGATIVE AFFECT

Either way, it's dangerous when news outlets try to capture our attention rather than present reality to us. It is extremely important to understand that not everything is as bad as it is often presented to us in a media cycle that thrives on sensationalism.

Unfortunately, we often forget how incredibly lucky we are to have been born in this day and age. The true state of the world can cautiously be described as: better than ever, maybe. Barack Obama famously said in 2017, "If you had to choose one moment in history in which to be born, and you didn't know in advance whether you were going to be male or female, which country you were going to be from, what your status was, you'd choose right now."

There are many metrics we can use to measure progress. But instead of writing a book on how great the world is, I will focus on just a few major changes that should make the case that there was likely no better time to be alive than right in this very moment.

Life Expectancy

One of the most obvious measures to gauge progress is life expectancy. Living longer is generally seen as a good thing, although one could argue that there's such a thing as too long. While I agree that some people suffer unnecessarily due to worsening health at an old age, it would be hard to argue that living shorter is better.

For example, I am thirty-three years old. Two centuries ago in the Netherlands, where average life expectancy was only forty years, I would have been safely considered an older man. The Netherlands was also the richest country at the time!

Today, there isn't a single country with a life expectancy that low. In 2019, American life expectancy was about seventy-nine years old. Despite the slight decline in recent years, it is still close to double what it was in the Netherlands two centuries earlier. I'd much rather live in a world where most of my adult life is in front of me rather than behind me.

Happiness

I understand that happiness isn't everything. I believe that we have to focus our lives away from indulging our short-term emotional and instinctual tendencies and toward long-term development and fulfillment. And we do some of that already when we make choices like having children or fighting for a noble cause. While momentary happiness isn't everything, happiness is a common metric to use when looking at a country's progress in the long run.

The World Happiness Report offers insights into the state of happiness around the globe.[39] The 2020 edition concludes that happiness scores in the top ten countries are more than twice as high than in the bottom ten. The researchers identified three main reasons for this disparity: GDP per capita, depth of social support, and life expectancy, each of which is highly correlated with happiness.

Speaking of life expectancy, people in countries with longer life expectancy have higher happiness levels. And so do people with depth of social support. Luckily, technology makes it easier than ever before to stay connected with distant loved ones, which might be why social support in the US has increased slightly over time.[40] People who feel lots of it are two to three times less likely to be depressed. Richer countries are also happier than poorer, and richer classes within countries are happier than poorer classes. There is overwhelming scientific evidence for each of those correlations.

But it is not all good news. While we are getting richer, living longer, and becoming happier overall, the world is not getting happier everywhere. The US especially is struggling; adult happiness in the US peaked in the 1990s, and it's been declining slowly since at least 2000.

Coincidentally, that's also when the adoption of broadband internet started. Don't get me wrong—I'm not arguing that broadband internet kills happiness. There actually is evidence that the opposite might be true. One study, for example, found that the internet has a positive influence on happiness, at least in European countries.[41]

Based on my research, it's hard to pinpoint what precisely leads to the US being an outlier. But my personal experience living in the US and several other countries has taught me that it might have to do with our overfocus on happiness.

The US is arguably the most fun-seeking culture in the world. We have Hollywood, Vegas, and Spring Break. But what if happiness can only be achieved in the long run by how we live our lives rather than how we escape through movies, vacations, and parties? If that's the case, we might be going about it all wrong in the US.

Another factor could be that the US, which birthed social media, is dealing with the damaging effects of its use on the happiness and self-image of adolescents.[42] There is also evidence showing that in-person friendships support happiness, while online connections don't, according to the World Happiness Report group. Additionally, smartphone usage is associated with lower levels of well-being, which could affect the happiness levels of the 95 percent of Americans who use them.[43]

That said, outside of the US, it's clear that the world is becoming a happier place, while factors like social media could be having an increasing negative impact. But more on that in Trend #3.

Exploration

It's easier than it's ever been to get around. As Steven Pinker, the author of Enlightenment Now, says, "Affordable transportation does more than reunite people... life is better when people can expand their awareness of our planet and species rather than being imprisoned within walking distance of their place of birth."

We can use our ability to see the world to explore new cultures and widen our horizons. And more people than ever are exploring our planet, at least when we are not living in total lockdown due to a virus. It's hard to say whether the COVID-19 pandemic will reduce our willingness to explore, but looking at data from 1995 to 2014, the cost of air travel came down significantly while the number of people flying increased. It's a classic example of how supply and demand works in combination with more disposable income.

More people flying means more freedom and exploration of the world. And even if exploration itself were not enough to make us happy, even the simple act of planning a vacation makes us happier.[44]

Knowledge

Knowing more is arguably better than knowing less. Sometimes ignorance is bliss, but in most cases, we prefer to know.

In the US in the late 1920s, less than 3 percent of fourteen- to seventeen-year-olds went to high school. By 2011, 80 percent of teenagers in that age group graduated from high school, and over two thirds ended up going to college. In 2015, almost a third of Americans held bachelor's degrees—more than went to high school in the 1920s.

Not only are Americans being better educated, they are also getting smarter. I know it's sometimes hard to believe when watching fail videos on YouTube, but it's true. For example, if the average teenager today with an IQ of 100 time-travelled back to 1950, they would have an IQ of 118—and an IQ of 130 in 1910. Only 2 percent of the population today has an IQ that high! This means that we are more knowledgeable and smarter than ever before, and young people are on average smarter than old people. Take that, grandma!

There are some exceptions, though. Some European nations have seen a recent slump in IQ scores.[45] Explanations range widely, but they include changes in educational exposure, worsening nutrition, and differences in media exposure. Yet again, the type of media we consume matters.

* * *

It's hard to imagine a better time to be alive than today. The progress humans have made, especially thanks to the internet, has been tremendous. We've increased opportunity, life expectancy, IQ scores, and opportunities to experience the world. The only exception might be happiness in the US, which has been declining over the past few decades. Nonetheless, the world has continued to grow richer, more accessible, and more enjoyable.

Objectively, things seem to be ticking upward. But the increasingly negative portrayal of the world in the media has influenced our perception of the state of the world. For example, based on an annual survey given to high-school seniors since 1975 by the University of Michigan, we know that twelfth graders today have a more pessimistic outlook than millennials had at the same age.[46] About 52 percent of twelfth graders think "things will get worse in the rest of the country in the next 5 years," while only 39 percent of millennials felt that way in 2001.

The negative media coverage is of course intentional; media companies simply understand human psychology based on our cave-inhabiting ancestors' needs. They know that we are more likely to click and read negative articles. And now that they have access to our phones, they can more easily deliver that content directly to us. All it takes is one single push notification, one beep or buzz, and we're drooling to unlock our smartphones.

In a famous experiment, a scientist and dog owner found that he could evoke a physical response in his dogs with a simple bell.[47] Every time it rang, the dogs started salivating because they knew it was time for a meal. Although compared to dogs, we have the autonomy to deactivate our phone notifications, most of us simply don't.

We allow companies direct access to our time, attention, and state of mind via our smartphones and other devices. This access allows those companies to share content that makes us believe that the world is a darker place than it truly is—and we get hooked on that feeling. How does that work? We will cover that in detail in the next chapter.

Key Takeaways

- The media represents the world more negatively than it did in the past.

- Quality of life has been increasing significantly over decades, and the world has, for the most part, become a better place to live in.

- Younger generations are more likely to think that the future will be worse than the present, although data has shown the opposite to be true.

- Because we are more likely to click on extreme content, media has become more negative to acquire more viewers. Consequently, we're becoming hooked on content that biases our view of the world.

TREND #3: EXTRACTIVE ALGORITHMS

In the past decade, I've been incredibly fortunate to work at some of my dream companies, bringing new technologies to market. At BMW, Lucid Motors, McKinsey, and Apple, I've had the opportunity to experience the leading automotive, consulting, and tech companies from the inside. While each company was essential for my learning and growth, none really challenged me and sparked as much personal and professional growth as did Apple, the birthplace of the smartphone and arguably the most successful hardware company our planet has ever seen.

In mid-2017, I was offered a job there as Worldwide Program Manager for New Product Introductions—a fancy title that essentially means helping Apple bring their newest gadgets to consumers by tracking people and their progress, making sure they do their work and launching products on time. It was a position that required previous experience in large, hardware-centric corporations and some well-developed people skills. It also required me to be available to Apple and on my devices every waking hour and, on some days, even sleeping hours.

I can't put into words the excitement I felt when the program management team at Apple offered me a role. I'd wanted to work for a large tech company in Silicon Valley since 2012 when I was in Germany at BMW. I remember the first time I visited the Valley. I signed up for a Silicon Valley guided bus tour to visit a few iconic tech companies and learn some facts, fun stories, and insights about them from our knowledgeable driver. I felt like a kid in a candy store.

When the tour bus arrived at Apple's then-headquarters in Cupertino, I felt a strong sense of belonging. When I think back to that day, clear images appear of Apple employees walking quickly in different directions as if their presence in their next meeting would determine the fate of the universe. I wanted to be part of that one day. Little did I know that just five years later, I'd leave BMW in Munich and start working for Apple in Cupertino.

I was super excited for this new chapter in my life. But, from day one as an insider, I found the company very different than I expected. Apple seemed like the American equivalent of BMW—another large, hierarchical corporation in which calling out others for mistakes seemed like every employee's highest purpose.

The people working at Apple's headquarters were special, though. I worked with some of the smartest and best-educated people I had ever worked with. Most of them had degrees from impressive universities and working experiences that others could only dream of. They were smart, hard working, and detail oriented.

Problems were approached with little emotion, analyzed in depth, and then reported through executive summaries up the hierarchy. It was easy to fall into the culture. Everybody was behaving and acting like they'd literally created this world. There was an omnipresent feeling that we were the best, and nothing could take us down. And to some degree, that might be true. Apple might actually be too important and too big to fail.

The iconic iPhone was for many people a masterfully engineered gateway to the internet—a black mirror that for over a decade has given us access to connection, convenience, and endless choice. Compared to its Android competitors, the iPhone's design, weight, and functionality have made it consistently more functional and simpler to use.

This might also explain why the average iPhone user engages with their phone for nine more hours in a given month than Android users do.[48] And iPhone users tend to engage with more content as well.

Our smartphones are the most powerful and compact tech devices in our lives. Never before have we carried a tool everywhere we go, even into our bathrooms, as if it were attached to us. In fact, maybe humans are no longer just a combination of body, mind and soul—maybe it's more accurate to say that we are now rather body, mind, soul, and phone. If the body connects us to the present physical reality around us, the mind projects us into the future, the soul carries the wisdom of the past, and our phone connects us to the timeless, internet-enabled reality of the digital world.

Our smartphones are our connection to each other's knowledge and lives. And with over 1.5 billion active devices worldwide, there is hardly another company that dictates our experience of the digital world as much as Apple does.

At Apple, everyone obviously uses iPhones, Macs, iPad, AirPods, and all the other great Apple products; unsurprisingly, Apple employees also hardly own other manufacturers' devices. They're also encouraged to own just one iPhone, meaning that one's personal and professional lives are "synced" and happen on the same device. Over time, it becomes hard to distinguish what is private or professional. You just start answering all messages at every time of the day.

And with that comes an expectation to be available most of the time. While my work was challenging at times, I feel lucky to say that I was—for the most part—"only" expected to be available during waking hours and only Monday through Friday. Other friends seemed to deal with seven-day-a-week work schedules.

Apple's culture is so unique and demanding that it either fits or doesn't fit with one's personality. Unfortunately, it wasn't the perfect fit for me. As excited as I was about the products that Apple put into the world, it became obvious to me six months in that I couldn't stay at Apple for very long. I wasn't willing to completely give up my personal interests and erase the boundaries between my private and professional life to have a chance at climbing the corporate ladder quickly.

About a year into working there, I fell into a depression, caused partly by the grueling work and commute, but more so from my increasing disconnection from the people who mattered to me and my growing connection with devices that couldn't provide me with the same level of happiness. This feeling was most pronounced while traveling on the corporate Apple buses that took commuters from San Francisco to Cupertino.

Although I shared over an hour's drive each way with my colleagues, we hardly ever talked on the bus. To some degree, the secretive culture at Apple and the fear of sharing confidential information with other employees seemed to prevent us from having any level of personal connection. It was easier to just stare at our smartphones the whole time than risk oversharing with another human.

So I ended up constantly connected to my Mac, iPad, iPhone, and Apple Watch while feeling more and more disconnected from myself and other humans. Only six months in, I already knew that the company's culture and the amount of time I spent on my devices was too much for my system to handle forever. I stuck it out for another two years because I wanted to learn more about Apple's secret sauce. But it cost me dearly.

After leaving Apple, I was the most physically and mentally unhealthy version of myself ever. The stress and always-on culture had drained me. Leaving Apple was the beginning of a slow recovery process, but it did not immediately heal me from overusing my iPhone. As we learned in the last chapter, higher smartphone usage is often associated with lower well-being, which drives users to escape even more fully into their phones. It was a vicious cycle that I was unaware of. Once I became aware of it, I started wondering what exactly my smartphone was doing that kept me wanting more even when it was clearly hurting me.

The Real Product

For a long time, futurists and other tech-savvy folk have feared a point in time when artificial intelligence would overwhelm humans' biological and cognitive strengths—when it would basically outsmart us. That point has been famously called the "technological singularity" or simply, the "singularity."

The term derives from mathematics and describes the point at which a given object cannot be defined or ceases to be well-behaved. Mathematically, it becomes harder to control for or measure an object like that. Over the past three decades, the term "Singularity" has become more popularized in regards to technology, driven predominantly by two thinkers: Vernor Vinge, a scientist and fiction writer, and Ray Kurzweil, a prominent futurist.

Vinge believed in 1993 that "within thirty years, we will have the technological means to create superhuman intelligence. Shortly after, the human era will end." Kurzweil agrees with this point of view, at least in principle, but thinks that the Singularity will occur around 2045 rather than in the 2020s. In his book *The Singularity Is Near*, Kurzweil describes an event caused by developments in artificial intelligence (AI) that will enable machines to become more intelligent than humans.

A smart AI could create systems that are beyond our capabilities to understand them, basically trapping us like a hamster in its wheel. At this point, we'd change from creators to slaves of an entity we'd created.

Many technologists fear that an AI would develop a desire to grow, learn, and improve itself, and might one day recognize humans as the biggest threat to its progress. And frankly, that would make sense for many reasons, especially when it comes to growth. Assuming that an AI desires growth just as much as humanity does, then its growth might be limited by our biological need to consume large amounts of energy through food and the earth's resources. Every day each one of us consumes three meals, drinks and wastes about forty gallons of water, and buys more goods online than we could ever use.

Our consumption is unsustainably depleting the planet's resources, putting at risk an AI's capability to expand itself. An AI with that information would understand that it either has to limit our hold on the planet or support our decimation.

Humans can only survive within narrow temperature ranges, eat a calorie-rich diet, and are prone to getting sick and even worse, old. An advanced virus, if produced by an AI, could quickly reduce our numbers. We also need a planet rich with water and an atmosphere that supports our survival. We have yet to physically step foot on another such planet, and likely won't for a long time.

Accelerating climate change could easily stop humanity from expanding further.

An AI probably wouldn't even need to go to such lengths. It would probably be easier to incentivize us to destroy ourselves. And to some degree, we're already doing this. We were fully capable of coming up with a system that puts little value on sustainable survival on planet earth ourselves: it's called capitalism. Unfortunately, it's likely the best economic system we currently have. But it inherently fails to account for limited resources like gasoline and water. And, as seen during the 2020 pandemic, economic incentives forced many politicians to place more value on economic stability than on human life or sustainability.

As an example, 780 million people still do not have access to a safe water source, and we're just nineteen years away from severe worldwide water shortages.

> "If Earth's history is represented in one single calendar year, modern humans have been around for just 37 minutes and managed to use up one third of Earth's natural resources in the last 0.2 seconds."

> - theworldcounts.com

The reality is, we are heavily resource constrained and continue to make our own circumstances more challenging. And while these constraints are expected to cause undesirable lifestyle changes for many of us in the future, AI and the wide application of algorithms are having a major influence on our behavior right now. Google searches, the Facebook feed, and YouTube recommendations literally dictate what we see, hear, click on, and ultimately react to.

Everybody using YouTube, Facebook, Twitter, or Google, which is the majority of people in the Western world, is influenced by their algorithms. The platforms decide for us what content we will be able to interact with based on what they think will keep us clicking, searching, and watching for the longest period of time.

How they decide to present information to us often is not in our best interest. Our Facebook feed information could be presented in a chronological way, showing us the most recent posts rather than ones chosen by the algorithm to keep us engaged. It could be organized around user-defined interests so you're more likely to see updates about something you truly care about rather than shocking posts from somebody you barely know.

Information can be organized in a multitude of ways. Unfortunately, we don't understand how modern media platforms organize information for us. Facebook and Google's algorithms are company secrets, and neither end users nor government officials understand all the incentives behind them—except that the companies want to keep us engaged for as long as possible.

A few people at the largest tech companies have the power to define what we see, hear, and react to on a global scale. This is not a conspiracy theory—it's just how tech works. Only a few people dictate what the masses experience. And while I'm not assuming malicious intent by any of the puppeteers at the top, there are obvious negative consequences that come with having publicly traded companies, who primarily serve shareholder interest, controlling information flow and ultimately our attention. The algorithms we are engaging with are catered not to the interest of the end users but to the interest of companies who strive to maximize profit and revenue while making shareholders happy.

Take Facebook and Google as prominent examples of content engines. Both companies rely heavily on advertising revenue for their business model. That means their purpose is to match advertisers with potential first-time or repeat customers. At their core, Google Search and Facebook are matchmakers for advertisers. Like Uber, which connects drivers with riders, Google and Facebook connect advertisers with consumers. They simply match supply with demand.

The demand side is straightforward to define: a customer, the advertiser, wants to buy access to information and people. They have the money, and they're willing to pay for the product. A lot of money, indeed. On the other side, the value being supplied is information about us. The supply is you and me.

Of course, Facebook is not just sending spreadsheets with basic demographic information and contact details to its advertising customers. The algorithms know so much more about us than we can imagine.[49] For example, they track our cookies, meaning they know what other websites we are visiting—which,

I would argue, is a pretty damn good way to guess our interests in life. Facebook also assigns every bit of content an individual score depending on how relevant Facebook thinks it is to you. The same content receives a different score for different humans, meaning the algorithm decides what you see or don't.

These companies also save our pictures, posts and all the other data we willingly give them every single day. We upload all of it for the best price possible: free of charge. Their product, our data and our attention, is essentially free of manufacturing cost, and their customers—ad companies—are willing to spend a lot of money for it.

Yes, of course they have some costs, like maintaining our data on their servers, upgrading those servers to ensure we can all be online at the same time, and keeping our data (somewhat) safe. That requires manpower and machine power, and it's certainly not cheap. But the product itself is essentially produced without any manufacturing costs.

That would be different if Facebook at least paid for our internet bill, but they don't. Imagine if Apple was producing iPhones at no cost and selling them for $999. The only cost Apple had was keeping their production facilities up to date and running. Apple's current net profit margins is about 21 percent, which is incredible for a (mostly) hardware company. BMW, a true hardware company, nets about 6.5 percent by comparison. But Apple's profit margin is nowhere near what a company like Facebook, with no per-unit cost, can achieve: about 34 percent as of 2020.[50] And no wonder—we essentially supply them with our data for free. To some degree, we all work for Facebook!

This means we're Facebook's product, and we're being treated as such. Profit-generating companies aim to sell their product at the highest possible value to their end customers. The product gets squeezed on every end: more features and reduced costs, to maximize the value for customers and thus charge them as much as possible. We are the product, and we are being optimized. It is the best way to increase our value to the real customer, advertisers.

Imagine you're an engineer at Facebook. You are called into a meeting with your boss, who says: "Mark asked me to find a way to improve our product because our profits have been dipping recently. We need to get users to spend more money. What should we do? How should we improve our algorithms to achieve that?" (This is more like an interview question at Facebook, rather than an actual question to an engineer, but let's roll with it.)

I can immediately think of three ways of achieving that goal.

First, we could get more users onto the platform. This would increase the quality of the product being sold to advertisers by giving them access to more people. Second, we could focus on having each user spend more time on the platform, even without delivering more value to the customer. Third, instead of keeping users on the platform for longer, we could attempt to get more information out of them while they're there. That means better tracking of how they behave online on and off our platform. Or present them with more information that they will engage with. Likes, shares, and comments are how the user interacts with Facebook and thus becomes a more defined product. The more Facebook knows, the better targeted the ads can be, the better the results for the advertiser, and the more money advertisers will want to spend.

And guess what? This is exactly what Facebook does. They suggest you add certain friends by mining your contacts, use endless scroll to keep you reading (and reading and reading), send all sorts of notifications to nudge you back onto the platform, and apply default settings that allow them to access more of your information than you might like. And what better platform to use for tracking our actions than the smartphones we carry wherever we go? Because your personal data is Facebook's business, it shouldn't come as a surprise that the company has been a target of privacy critiques for several years.[51]

In short, more people spending more time more deeply engaged is what social media and search engine platforms are optimizing for. They're not in the business of delivering the highest value product to us—they're in the business of extracting value from us. The most obvious way to do that is to create extractive algorithms to do the job in real time. We don't have to wait until the Singularity—you and I are already a product whose behavior is, at least to some degree, directed by machines.

How does that work, you might ask? Let's get into it.

Algorithms Are Powerful, and So Are We

What makes algorithms extractive is the fact that they serve us what they expect we're most likely to engage with. And we're most engaged with content when it's controversial.

Facebook and Twitter thrive on controversy because it is more likely to go viral. We saw this in the 2016 election. Whether or not Donald Trump won because of Russian interference is not the point. What we do know is that a lot of politically targeted fake content was created in 2016 to engage with users, go viral, and sway as many people as possible.

The creators didn't care if the content was true or fictional. What mattered is that it was inflammatory enough to get people to click on it. But don't just trust me—listen to Bruce Ableson, the inventor of Open Diary, considered the first online blogging community and thus the first social networking site.

In a podcast on Community Signal, Ableson describes the Facebook feed of 2016 as "this horrible self-feeding mechanism where untrue or inflammatory content was boosted and boosted and boosted. And they haven't really done a lot to fix that since then. I mean, they obviously know about it. And they've made a bunch of sort of pseudo moves to fix it. But I don't think it'll ever be perfect as long as it's driven by money that's connected to click rate."[52]

The result of all of this product optimization is that we, the product, are fed inflammatory information because we react to it the most. We are being constantly improved to be worth more in the eyes of advertisers and content producers. Unfortunately, feeding targeted or inflammatory information to users influences the decisions we make in real life.

> "Medieval institutions and godlike technologies. This is kind of the problem statement of humanity."
>
> - **Tristan Harris**, director, Center for Humane Technology

Tristan, one of my brightest friends and someone who has been called the "closest thing Silicon Valley has to a conscience" by the *Atlantic*, spent three years at Google as a Design Ethicist. He developed a framework for how technology should ethically steer the thoughts and actions of billions of people, but you might know him better as the guy behind the Netflix documentary *The Social Dilemma.*

At the Center for Humane Technology, he's working on reversing the effects of what he calls "human downgrading," which is when our capabilities to process and understand the world around us are being reduced due to factors like information overload, addictive use of tech, mass narcissism, fake news, polarization, bots, and deep fakes.

In early 2019, about a month before Tristan officially presented his mission to some of the most powerful technologists and politicians in the US, he came over to my house for dinner. He explained to me his conviction that exponential technology is taking advantage of basic, ancient human instincts that can't resist the incentives created by exploitive technologies.

Tristan compared the way these technologies work to the way magicians perform their tricks. Magic, in one sense, is the study of the limits of the evolutionary features of our minds. Magicians understand the limitations of our minds. When they perform, they know our shared blind spots precisely and take advantage of them through their actions, body language, and words. As technologists further their understanding of the human mind, they, like magicians, develop programs specifically targeting these instincts with the goal of affecting people's attention and actions. Large technology companies do that with billions of people.

He calls this process of extracting value from our basic instincts the "race to the bottom of the brain stem"—essentially reverse-engineering those instincts to create the world's most sophisticated magic trick, influencing people's actions without their realizing it and hooking us to the process of being exploited.

We've all at some point ended up in a YouTube, Instagram, or TikTok wormhole, expecting a playful five-minute scrolling experience only to find ourselves wasting forty-five minutes. When we put down our phones we sometimes feel like a drug addict coming off a high, like a flow state has been taken away and replaced with an unsavory reality.

This loss of control is not only real—it's intentional. Every time you open a YouTube video, the recommendation engine is waiting for your next decision. Every time you make a decision, it creates an even better replica of your behaviors in their system, one that predicts your next move. After a while, it likely knows your subconscious mind and instincts better than you do. That is the power of exploitive algorithms.

The proof that this is happening is in the data. Tristan presented one of the most persuasive pieces of evidence in April 2019 in his "New Agenda for Tech", based on research he'd done on the influence of controversial topics and extreme world views on human attention.[53]

The piece in the Agenda that stood out to me was on flat-earth theory.

Since extreme viewpoints are more engaging—things like Bigfoot, UFOs, and flat earth theory—Tristan's hypothesis was that YouTube recommendation engines would prefer them. So Tristan and the team at the Center for Humane Technology looked at flat earth theory to test their hypothesis. They found that in 2017, about 20 percent of Google searches on flat earth favored the theory. On YouTube, the number was bigger: 35 percent. But it gets really interesting when you look at YouTube recommendations. Tristan and his team discovered that if you watched a flat earth video, YouTube would recommend more videos in favor of the theory 90 percent of the time.

It's easy to believe in a theory when it's the only one around. When 90 percent of what we see favors an extreme theory by every credible scientist, when information is provided to make us dependent rather than happy or fulfilled, when we get unconsciously sucked into rabbit holes, it's clear that extractive algorithms bend our perception of free will in their desired direction. The extractive attention economy is attacking our ability to choose how we want to spend our time. It's downgrading our identities and our attention spans, and increasing our biases.[54]

Guillaume Chaslot, a former YouTube developer and founder of Algo-Transparency, a project that seeks greater transparency from online platforms, claims that YouTube's algorithm "isn't built to help you get what you want—it's built to get you addicted to YouTube. Recommendations were designed to waste your time."[55] He thinks that "right now the incentive is to create this type of borderline content that's very engaging, but not forbidden."

All of this might scare you, and it is certainly alarming. Whether or not you believe that social media is depleting our free will or downgrading us as human beings, at the end of the day, we still have autonomy and need to take responsibility for our lives. What if the numbers above are just a warning sign to act? You might feel helpless, but acting helplessly doesn't serve you. In parts II and III, we will talk about how to take responsibility, unlock your curiosity, and learn tools that will help you regain control of your digital world.

Until then, let me say this: social media can sway your opinions if you don't recognize how you might be maneuvering yourself into them. For example, Kyrie Irving, one of the best point guards in basketball, brought himself to believe that flat-earth theory was true, at least for a little while. He attributed this to some late nights he spent bored, clicking through YouTube recommendations. He made his belief public, and although he retracted it soon thereafter, unfortunately, some of his millions of followers were likely swayed and continued spreading the theory.

At the end of 2020 I spoke to Nir Eyal, who spent years researching the field of digital distractions about his views on social media and the effects of extractive algorithms. He believes that social media companies like Facebook have an incentive to make us believe that their powerful algorithms can in fact manipulate us.

Just like cigarette manufacturers have profited from making us believe that we can't stop smoking because smoking is so addictive (and so we shouldn't even try), social media companies are trying to convince us that we can't stop scrolling because their algorithms have power over us. This narrative is helpful to companies like Facebook because people are less likely to reduce their time online after they give up the belief that it is possible.

Nir and I believe that this narrative serves us users as well. It gives us a scapegoat, something to put blame onto when we have a hard time explaining what is really going on. For example, you might believe that our fellow citizens voted for the wrong president because ads on social media told them to do so, but obviously the reality is much more complex than that. "It's an easy answer to a complex problem," Nir says, and I agree.

And it helps Facebook ensure that their supply (your time) stays online.

There is a demand side to this equation as well. Social media companies that are based on an advertising model—which is most of them—have to ensure that advertisers trust their ability to not only get in front of the right person but also influence that person to click on it. What would it say about Facebook if they were to admit that they cannot influence people's purchasing behavior more than other platforms might be able to? "That's the catch 22. Even if they wanted to tell us that their algorithms are not quite that powerful, they really can't out of self interest," Nir explains.

Don't get me wrong—Facebook and other social media companies have a major influence on our lives. Their algorithms clearly have some power to influence our behaviors. There is no doubt about that. But just imagine for a second that they weren't quite as powerful. Would Facebook come out and tell us that?

There is another reason I believe there is incentive to keep social media's bad guy image alive: politicians benefit from it, too. It gives them permission to act on it, creating new regulations, and it gives more power to the government to influence and restrict the workings of social media platforms. We know that regulation can help, but whether or not it will help is entirely up to how it is implemented.

What remains true is that the use of social media has a negative impact on younger generations who have not yet developed coping mechanisms to prevent tech overload. A Pew Research Center survey in March 2020 reported that 70 percent of teenagers think that depression is a problem among their peers.[56] And some researchers suggest that the growing amount of time teens are spending on social media is contributing to the growth in anxiety and depression among this group.[57]

On the surface, it also looks like young people's ability to focus has been downgraded. Some studies report that Gen Z's attention span is eight seconds, down from millennials' twelve seconds.[58] And by the way, a goldfish is reported to have a nine-second attention span.

This sounds bad, but maybe it isn't. What if this is how Gen Zers are attempting to protect their emotional and mental well-being, by simply spending less of their attention? Rather than being downgraded, maybe it's actually a protective mechanism?

Digital technologies can be used to sharpen our cognitive abilities. Neurology professor Adam Gazzaley believes that "mobile technology can be harnessed to improve our minds." Other researchers believe that some games can create children with better reasoning skills.[59]

At least until politicians introduce functional regulation of social media companies, it's up to us to decide how to use technology, because it's possible to use these powerful tools responsibly. While the trends are alarming, we have the power to reverse them.

Alternatively, if we continue at the current rate, we will spend five years and four months of our lives on social media.[60] And that is assuming no growth in social media consumption! It's up to you to be responsible with the gateway to your attention—your smartphone—as well as the apps on it and the notifications you set for them. You have to, because nobody else will. Nobody else can.

Key Takeaways

- We are not the customers of social media companies—we are their products.

- Extreme viewpoints are more likely to cause engagement and are therefore propagated by social media companies.

- Human downgrading is the result of social media companies optimizing us, their product, by hooking us through their algorithms beyond our own interest to engage with them.

- Depression rates have been rising over the past decade, especially among teenagers and young adults; some researchers believe this is connected to the rise of social media.

TREND #4: ABUNDANCE OF CHOICE

Choice is abundant in modern society. Wherever we look, there are more options than our minds can process.

An Amazon search for a smartphone charging dock turns up more than four thousand results. Open Tinder or any other dating app in a major city and you'll be presented with more potential partners than you could ever connect with. And on Netflix, the number of options is so overwhelming that we often give up; the value of whatever we watch is less than the pain of choosing the right title. Tech has made endless options available to us, but do we actually want them?

While getting my MBA at UC Berkeley, I had the pleasure of learning from and tutoring classes for Prof. Don Moore. He is one of the world's leading researchers in decision making focused on leaders and executives who have to make difficult decisions that influence many people. From him, I learned how to optimize the outcome of a decision (which I am pretty good at outside of gaming/gambling) and prevent myself from feelings of regret for having chosen incorrectly.

In decision-making theory, there is an observed phenomenon called the paradox of choice. Barry Schwartz, an American psychologist, defined the term in his book *The Paradox of Choice: Why More is Less*. Schwartz observed that having many options to choose from, while an inherent desire for most of us, is actually making us less happy. Schwartz states that having an overabundance of options can actually lead to anxiety, indecision, paralysis and dissatisfaction.[61]

Even if you haven't yet heard of this term, I'm sure you've experienced it. When there are many different events to choose from, a dozen versions of the same product on Amazon, or too many restaurants to order takeout from, we get overwhelmed.

At the same time, we like having choices. Who would say that they want fewer options? Having more options not only makes us feel safer but also gives us the impression that we are more likely to get exactly what we want.

The problem is, our desire for options is misaligned with the fact that we often struggle to make decisions. Some people struggle more, others struggle less, but we all need time and effort to make good decisions. So why do we desire more choice when it costs us resources to decide?

Choice gives the impression of freedom and personalization, but the effort required to make a decision often leads to anxiety and uncertainty about whether we've chosen wisely.

The desire for more choice and the effort of choosing work against each other. If the two are not negatively correlated, then at least at a certain point the relationship between choice and happiness shifts from positive to an inverse one. We know that people who are overwhelmed by choice can become more anxious and avoid making a choice altogether. I believe that avoidance can lead to self-blame and a downward spiral of unhappiness.

So what do we optimize for—more choice, or conserving our decision-making resources? Which option is better? How do we maximize our happiness?

Schwartz argues that the "secret to happiness is to have low expectations." While I agree, it seems like he is only tackling one side of the coin. On one side is a reduction of expectations, but on the other side is the reduction of resources needed to make decisions. I would argue that the secret to making better decisions is to make decisions less frequently and thus limit the resources that go into making decisions every day.

Our brains are like processing units, similar to the CPUs in our smartphones. Like my smartphone, my brain is sometimes really slow to compute things. And the reason for that is the same reason that your smartphone is sometimes slow: we have too many apps open at the same time, draining computational resources. If you worry about many things at work and home, and have to make several decisions throughout the day, chances are that you are running many background tasks constantly.

Researchers at the University of Oregon discovered that our memory has a limited capacity to juggle multiple concepts, ideas, and words at the same time. The average person may only be able to hold four things in their minds at once.[62] The part of the brain responsible for holding that information is called working memory and can be simply understood as the sketchbook of the mind. That is where our brain simultaneously holds numbers, names, and other information in the short term to perform mental tasks such as problem solving.

The basic idea here is that our ability to choose from options is correlated with our working memory capacity. Getting back to the smartphone example, this means that we can only have three or four apps open at the same time, while the rest are running in the background. The background apps can be opened more quickly than if they were fully closed, but they are not accessible while we have the three or four primary apps running. Our minds are great tools. Juggling four items at once already is impressive, so let's not overwhelm ourselves with too much choice.

Cognitive neuroscientists know that most of our cognitive activity is hidden from our conscious mind. We are aware of only about 5 percent of it, so most of our thoughts, emotions, and behaviors rely on the 95 percent of brain activity that doesn't reach our conscious awareness.[63] Most of the several thousand thoughts we have every day go unnoticed! Siegmund Freud already believed that the unconscious mind does most of the work daily.

Whether it's our unconscious or conscious mind making a decision for us, there is mental effort involved. Combined with the fact that our minds can only hold only four things at once, it becomes clear that making decisions is difficult and draining. Let me give you an example of how even seemingly easy choices can overwhelm us.

Overwhelmed by Seemingly Simple Decisions

As you know, I joined Apple as a Program Manager for New Product Introductions in 2017. One of the problems I had with Apple from the beginning was how far away the campus was from my home in San Francisco. It took me anywhere from sixty to ninety minutes door to door, depending on when I took off.

Apple's shuttle buses came so frequently that it felt like an endless number of options to choose from. Between 6:00 am and 10:30 am, tech buses literally took over San Francisco streets.

In 2018, I took a different bus almost every day. Every evening I would set my alarm for a different time depending on when I went to bed, what my meeting schedule looked like, how tired I expected to be, and frankly, when I wanted to get into work. It required research and self understanding. But mostly it required computing power. My brain was looking for the optimal solution, and it feared that it wouldn't get it right.

"No big deal," I'd think. "It's just a tiny little decision every night before I go to bed. How bad can that be?"

Pretty bad, to be honest. It took me many minutes to make that decision each night when I was already super tired and not capable of making the best decisions. I often had to buffer extra time in case the bus was a little early or I was too tired. By the beginning of 2019, I was so fed up with making this decision every day that although I still believed that it gave me more freedom, I gave in.

I realized that having to make this decision every evening was making me less happy, so I changed my approach. For the rest of 2019, my alarm went off at the same time every day: 6:12 am. I took the same 6:45 am bus for an entire year. And I did not confront myself with the bus decision paradox I had struggled with.

The consequences of this decision were surprisingly positive. Not only was my commute time reduced by an average of fifteen minutes, but I had more time to get work done, and I was sleeping better. Plus, I didn't have to worry about missing the bus or dealing with a bad driver. (The 6:45 am driver was incredible.) And my brain felt a little faster and had a little more endurance. Paradoxically, giving up choice actually resulted in more freedom!

Eliminating one decision that drained my computing power every evening increased my happiness levels and decreased my anxiety. Now imagine the potential impact of reducing the number of decisions in other areas of your life, like whether to brush your teeth or shower first, what clothes or shoes to wear, what to make for breakfast, or which work item to tackle first.

Most of us have too many apps running in the background, draining our batteries and reducing our computing speed. There is less energy to focus on the only app that matters—the one in the foreground. The solution to this problem could lie in choice and frequency reduction.

Some of us, however, deal better with having many choices. One of my friends is excellent at knowing what to choose in moments when I am already feeling a choice paralysis. She developed that skill very early in her childhood. But most of us do not consciously work on our ability to make decisions. And what is even worse, most parents teach us to be bad decision makers, which has repercussions on how we interact with technology as adults. Let me explain.

The four most commonly identified parenting styles, according to Amy Morin, a psychotherapist and international bestselling author, are "authoritarian," "permissive," "uninvolved," and "authoritative."[64] Each style takes a different approach to upbringing and can be identified by a number of characteristics that significantly shape children's behavior. According to Morin's research, three of these four styles lead to children having lower self-esteem, less ability to accept and understand what they want and children who make worse decisions.

Authoritarian parents, for example, are famous for saying, "Because I said so," when a child questions the reasons behind a rule. Children who grow up under the regime of strict authoritarian parents tend to be rule followers, but their obedience comes at a high price. They are at greater risk of developing self-esteem problems because their actions were valued more than their opinions as kids.

Permissive parents typically take an approach of being equals. They often prefer a friend role over a parent role and thus encourage their children to talk with them about their problems. This may sound great, but permissive parents, like friends, won't always keep you from making bad decisions. Kids who grow up with permissive parents are more likely to struggle academically, often have lower self-esteem, and report a lot of sadness.

Uninvolved parents expect children to raise themselves. They don't devote much time or energy into meeting their kids' needs. Often they are just overwhelmed with their own problems and as a consequence make their children feel left out. Children often desire a deeper connection, but the need is unmet. Children with uninvolved parents are likely to struggle with self-esteem issues, perform poorly in school, and rank low in happiness.

Finally, authoritative parents set up rules and explain the reasons behind them. They enforce those rules and give consequences. They take the child's feelings into consideration. Researchers have found kids who have authoritative parents are most likely to become responsible adults who feel comfortable expressing their opinions. Kids who grew up this way are more likely to be able to make good decisions.

If you weren't raised by authoritative parents, chances are you're not that good at making decisions, knowing yourself, or being comfortable in your own skin! And the recent rise of helicopter parenting hasn't made it easier for kids to find their own way, either. So how do we make good decisions in an increasingly complex world when we grew up overwhelmed by the need to choose or with parents who took our decision-making authority from us?

Technology is overwhelming us with choices left and right. Some of us have a downgraded ability to make decisions because of our parents' upbringing, but everyone is bombarded with an overwhelming amount of choice through digital media. Tech is overwhelming our already weak ability to choose.

On top of all of that, as if choosing wasn't difficult enough, we are full of biases. According to Don Moore, at least "one of these (biases) arises from the limitations on human memory and data collection. The availability bias leads us to overestimate the frequency or likelihood of events that are more memorable or salient."[65] We overestimate how likely events that happened recently are to happen again, meaning we more often than not make decisions based on recent experiences. Other inherent biases lead us to overvalue the opinions of people similar to us and to overestimate our capabilities.

And finally, our ability to mentally handle only three or four items at once puts us at odds with our devices' capacity to store and recall large quantities of information.[66] We designed computers with memories we wish we had. While machines have the ability to store all information for future usage, without losing any details, we humans simply cannot. We have to rely on a combination of murky memories, information stored in our DNA inaccessible by our conscious mind, and the belief systems we hold to make decisions.

If we can only remember that many things at once, wouldn't it make sense to limit our choices to four items or fewer by either reducing the number of choices or the frequency of making them? Try this out next time you buy something online: Stop your research at the fourth item you find that fulfills your needs. Decide among the four, and live happily ever after…

But I'm getting ahead of myself. We'll talk about solutions in parts II and III of the book. Next up is the topic of convenience: how tech is fostering it and its consequences on our lives.

Key Takeaways

- Choice gives the impression of freedom and personalization, but the effort required to make a decision often leads to anxiety and uncertainty about whether we've chosen wisely.

- Most parents do not support our development of healthy decision-making skills.
- The average person may only be able to hold four things in their minds at once.
- Reducing the number of choices and frequency of decision making might actually give us more freedom and happiness.

TREND #5: CONVENIENCE ECONOMY

What became clear to me during my time at Apple was that the devices we made were not only beautiful and elegant, they were also literal freedom machines for so many employees and users. This is especially true for the iPhone. It frees us from physical limitations and helps us connect to each other in strikingly convenient ways.

And Apple is not the only tech company working to free us from physical constraints. Amazon connects producers and creators with customers. Uber connects drivers with passengers. Facebook connects people who want to share their lives with people who want to follow those lives.

In this process of becoming unbound from physical constraints, tech companies have created an abundance of choice and unprecedented convenience. We are connected to goods, services, information, and other humans more closely than ever before.

That connection is also hastening the dematerialization of our lives. We no longer have to buy CDs to get music delivered to our phones, we can see each other without being in person, and we can stay up to date through a single app instead of buying printed newspapers. Material things are turning into ones and zeros made available to all of us, conveniently.

I truly believe that the internet is humanity's greatest development. For the first time, we are connected globally, cheaply, and instantaneously. By most metrics, the development of internet-based tech has been an outstanding stepping stone to true connection amongst humans—and it's been financially rewarding, too.

For example, a 2012 study finds that increasing mobile phone adoption in developing countries by 10 percent would increase productivity by over 4 percent.[67] There is direct personal financial benefit from having access to information and people through our phones. The internet has enabled optimization on a scale never seen before. We can do more with fewer resources—or at least, do what we already do more easily.

Consequently, most tech engineers are no longer the revolutionary thinkers of the nineties, but detail-oriented optimizers who thrive on making things faster and more convenient. I experienced it myself working at an electric car start-up, then later for Apple. Most of my colleagues were extremely hard working, smart, and detail oriented. But only a couple would I describe as visionary.

It's hard to find true innovators at big tech companies nowadays. Many of us have been complaining about Apple's lack of innovation or Facebook's inability to adjust to social needs. But what the tech companies remain excellent at is optimization for the sake of convenience.

From two-day delivery to same-day delivery to two-hour delivery, Amazon has shown us how to play that convenience game right. We can order every imaginable item on Amazon, many of which are available within a couple of hours. This would have been unimaginable only fifteen years ago!

But the convenience afforded by the internet is also a one-way street. Once we get used to it, it's very difficult to give up. Once you started using a washing machine, could you really go back to washing laundry by hand? Once Amazon started delivering household items, could you really go back to driving for thirty minutes to buy them? After you first experienced access to video streaming, would you be willing to wait for a DVD to arrive in the mail? Or why visit a library for answers when Google Search is at your fingertips?

I believe convenience is one of the most underrated forces in our lives. When we are asked to give up privacy for convenience, most of us do it in a heartbeat (when sharing on social media, for example). Convenience makes it so easy to shop for anything that we often don't question whether we need that thing in the first place. Convenience biases us to focus only on the obvious surface benefit, the part that meets our immediate needs. How or why the product was created or delivered doesn't really matter.

Convenience can also be dehumanizing. Your phones make you equally accessible to humans and bots, 24/7. Convenient, but problematic.

"In today's hyperconnected world, convenience is the ultimate currency." - **Nielsen Research**, 2018

In a 2018 report titled, "The Quest for Convenience," the Nielsen research company identifies six drivers for the increasing global demand for ease, utility, and simplicity.[68] Unsurprisingly, the uptake of technology is one of them. The more technology drives convenience, the more convenient we want things to be. As a result, we are changing our physical activity, dietary habits, and social behaviors. We crave convenience—but not all of it is bad. Technology gives us more time to pursue meaningful experiences as well. Whether that is philanthropic work or simply more time spent with the people we love, convenience gives us back time.

And I cherish the time that has been given to me (for the most part). I have tried and failed at giving up some of the conveniences of life, too. A few years ago, I wanted to downsize and give up on conveniences with the goal of living a more humane life. So I decided to make a drastic lifestyle change that would support that decision.

Inconveniences of #VanLife

In 2017, I bought my first camper van. It was an old Chevy G30 High Top that my girlfriend and I lovingly called "our fat child Grant" (although the vehicle was ten years older than me). Grant was well into his forties, but had a little fat boy smile. He was also an adventurer that wanted to explore the National Forests. From Yosemite to Burning Man, Grant was a solid and reliable companion who was also well known by our friends.

Grant's only problem was that he was a hard drinker. With an average consumption of nine miles per gallon, the gasoline cost to drive to Burning Man and back from San Francisco was about $400. Nevertheless, Grant made 2018 the favorite year of my life. Every other weekend we were out and about staying in different forests, attached to nature and detached from other humans. We were often able to work from home on Fridays, which meant leaving early in the morning and then working from our camper van as long as there was reception.

I associated myself with #vanlife, a movement that was becoming increasingly popular with young adults who wanted to free themselves from the constraints of living in a city in a small apartment, paying horrendous rents just to survive. They were people who wanted to live a minimal, less convenient lifestyle. And most of them were people who were wealthy enough to make #vanlife a choice.

For me, #vanlife seemed like a way to experience a new freedom and save money at the same time. If you've never heard of it, a few minutes searching this hashtag on Instagram will reveal scenes of nature, beauty, relaxation, fun, and freedom. The dream of living in a van is comparable to the dream our parents' generation associated with a convertible. #Vanlife is the millennial version of the convertible, and I was lucky enough to be able to afford to try it out.

After two years of truly memorable experiences vacationing with Grant, my partner and I decided to upgrade to a $50,000 Mercedes Sprinter camper van and move in full time. I felt so privileged to be able to afford myself the Mercedes-Benz of camper vans. Being able to uproot and live a #vanlife was a privilege that also taught me some unexpected lessons about myself and the comfort of basic conveniences.

At the end of 2019, we moved into our new van. The first few days were kind of fun. We explored our newly bought van, celebrated our liberation from our home, and got excited about making trips into the nearby National Forests. We even planned a four-month trip to Guatemala and agreed to learn Spanish together. The dream of having a van became reality, and the freedom seemed endless. And the van seemed perfect. We had running water, solar cells on the roof, a nice fridge, and the ability to cook with gas or electricity.

It truly had everything we would have wanted in a van … except space and any conveniences. And while the idea of having a van seemed so freeing, life in it soon became a burden. Problems arose almost immediately:

- Where do you have Amazon packages sent when you no longer have a physical address?

- How do you wash your clothes when you no longer have a washer and dryer?

- How do you regulate temperature in a metal space smaller than most people's bathrooms?

- How do you poop comfortably in the same space you eat and work while your partner is there?

- How do you stay productive when your partner wants to cook and there isn't enough space to do two things at once?

- Where do you shower, and how long does it take you to get clean, when the nearest shower is usually miles rather than feet away?

- Where do you dump your pee and poop legally after the camper toilet fills up?

- Where do you park at night, safely and evenly, to prevent worrying or sleeping at an angle?

Honestly, the list of inconveniences was endless. At one point I wrote them all down and calculated how much extra time I was spending every day on inconveniences I previously hadn't needed to deal with. It averaged out to about an extra hour of chores every day. And I'm not even counting the lost sleep at nights while the rain was pouring down on our metal home or the endless hours spent worrying about parking safely, legally, and unsuspiciously.

In summary, life in a van is hard — very hard. And so is giving up on conveniences. It didn't feel worth it to me to give up an hour per day on inconveniences. An hour might not sound like that much, but it's an hour of chores. Would you want to sort out the dishwasher or clean your home for an extra hour per day? Those are not very fun activities.

The pain I felt from giving up so many conveniences, amongst some other unfortunate circumstances, turned into a small, short-lived depression in January. Eventually, I had to ask a friend if I could stay at his apartment alone for a few days to recuperate. My friend had left for Europe for a couple of weeks, so his apartment was empty, and I hardly left during the five days I was there. The experience of living in our van with a partner had given me an endless appreciation for the conveniences of modern housing.

I learned about my boundaries around space. Mostly I discovered that there's always room for more conveniences, but it's hard to go back and reduce them without inflicting pain on oneself. It can also be healing to let go of some conveniences, and the experience in my first camper van was a great example of that. Letting go of a few conveniences for an extended weekend felt super liberating. But giving up on many modern ones as a lifestyle felt burdensome. I seemed to enjoy #vancation, not #vanlife.

My partner and I were so unhappy with #vanlife that between January and March, we spent most nights at friends' places instead of in the van. The burden of not having a home was real. I had an idealized expectation of what it would be like to give up the conveniences to which I had grown accustomed — afforded to me by the privilege of being financially secure. I can't believe I ever thought that not having a house would be easy!

It took us another two months to get back into living in an actual house long term. And boy, was I happy to have a proper home, shower, and kitchen appliances. Having roommates again with whom I could share space, laughter, and maybe most importantly, chores with, felt newly liberating. My life became exciting again, after I was able to regain the conveniences I'd become used to.

Some conveniences are useful, while others are not. But all of them can create dependency!

The instant availability of just about anything we need, plus the ability to outsource tasks we don't enjoy, like washing dishes in a dishwasher, saves a ton of time. My experience living in a van made it clear that I could give up on some conveniences. I don't really need a dishwasher. I might be okay without a dryer. But convenience, when it comes to hot showers and running water, absolutely helps us live fulfilling lives. So what's the right balance? Until what point does convenience have a net positive effect, and when does our dependence on it start to hinder our ability to live fulfilling lives?

Convenience, Withdrawal, and Consequences

The experience of removing certain elements of our luxurious modern lives caused withdrawal symptoms. I refused to adjust to the new, less convenient lifestyle and was constantly bothered by the loss of ease and comfort. The modern tech world has accustomed us to work-saving appliances and internet-based technologies that provide us with instant everything: instant food delivery, instant answers to all of our questions, and instant loneliness relief. And in this instant-everything economy, faster still seems to be better.

But convenience comes at a significant cost. The exact nature of that cost depends on whom you ask. A financial guru would say that convenience impacts our bank accounts negatively. According to research from 2019 commissioned by Ladder and conducted by OnePol, the average American spends $18,000 on non-essentials every year.[69] When looking at conveniences alone, a study by finder.com estimates their cost to be closer to $4,000 per year.[70] Obviously, there is nothing wrong with enjoying a few luxuries, but Americans are spending a small fortune on them.

An environmentalist might say that convenience increases packaging and plastic waste. Nearly half of all plastic ever produced has been made since the year 2000.[71] And most packaging is single-use; for everything that's contained, the container is waste. I experienced this cost as a PM at Apple. To compete with Amazon's industry-leading delivery speeds, we had to ask our logistics partners for faster deliveries that inflated their carbon footprint.

Right now, profit incentives are pushing retailers in the wrong direction and into a vicious cycle. Instant shipping encourages consumers to make more frequent smaller purchases. Rather than waiting for a single, large purchase that may seem cumbersome and challenging, customers order items whenever they think of a need. As of 2019, three in four Americans shopped online, about one in three Americans got at least one package delivered per week, and 77 percent said that free shipping was important to their decision.[72] [73] While it doesn't cost us much to ship something, the environment pays for it through emissions, packaging, and waste.

And finally, a fitness guru might say that convenience atrophies our physical bodies and has a negative impact on our energy levels. The level to which we are willing to automate our lives to prevent taking an extra physical step is reaching comical levels. Do we really need an Alexa-enabled TV that turns on when we call it, instead of taking the extra step to pick up the remote? Less than a quarter of Americans are meeting all national physical activity guidelines, according to a 2018 report from the Centers for Disease Control and Prevention's National Center for Health Statistics (NCHS).[74] Convenience is literally making us physically sick.

And it shows up in other data, too. Life expectancy in the US has been steadily declining in the past few years.[75] In the first half of 2020 alone, US life expectancy dropped by a full year according to a report from the National Center for Health Statistics.[76] A full year in just six months! Obviously deaths from COVID-19 are the main factor when looking at 2020, but the overall trend is caused by mental and physical health-related issues among working-age Americans. Obesity-related mortality rates among twenty-five to sixty-four-year-olds went up by 114 percent! Suicide rates went up by nearly 40 percent between 1999 and 2017.

This is the misery of the wealthiest and most powerful country in the world. We're dying earlier than we did in the past, and outrageously convenient tech might be contributing to it.

How much convenience is helpful, and when does it become harmful to our mental, emotional, and physical well-being? I'm not sure where to draw the line, but I know for certain the net effect of the convenience economy depends on how we use the services provided to us! If used correctly, technology enables us to do more of what we want to do by conveniently reducing what we don't desire.

But also consider this: if you focus on working out some of your muscles while avoiding training others—many buff guys really don't like working out their legs in gyms—the parts you work out will become stronger and the ones you neglect will become weaker. As a whole, we are only as strong as our weakest link.

In a similar way, we have to be conscious about how we choose our conveniences. We will choose the convenient route much of the time because we're human, but conveniences can cause imbalances by atrophying certain parts of our being and strengthening others. As our smartphones have become the most convenient, powerful tool in our lives, we have to be especially conscious about making choices related to the use of these devices that serve us in becoming the balanced person we want to be. We will talk about just how to do that in part III.

Key Takeaways

- Conveniences create dependencies and stop us from questioning whether we really need something in the first place. To some degree, they replace care with ease.

- That said, giving up too many conveniences at once can feel depressing. Adding a convenience is easy, but removing one is hard.

- Among the potentially negative environmental and financial impacts, convenience also has a negative impact on our physical health—less than a quarter of Americans are getting enough physical activity.

- Conveniences can either help make us even more human by removing chores and giving back time to connect with others, or they can downgrade us.

- We will accept very high costs for our convenience and we will choose conveniences that are available to us consistently—whether or not they are helping us achieve our goals.

UNDERSTANDING THE TRENDS

We live in a complex and uncertain world. It makes us want to literally hold onto things like our smartphones, grasp after experiences that feel controllable, and focus on satisfying present-moment urges. But at the same time, humanity as a whole has never prospered more. There is a reason why many scientists and leaders like Barack Obama call this the best time in history to be alive. These are complex and prosperous times.

At the same time, the media has become more negative. We're guided to think that the world is a worse place than it actuallyis because we read that it is, every single day. And if the media hasn't scared you enough with its sensationalistic reporting, then the major tech companies' extractive algorithms will insert themselves into your remaining sane mental space. These algorithms know who you are, what you've looked at, and what you're more likely to click on.

"We don't watch what we want to see; we watch what we can't help but look at."

- **Michaela Carmein**, software engineer at Patreonand brainstorming wizard for the Center for Humane Technology

The complexity of the world, increasingly negative media sentiment, and tech companies' extractive algorithms combine to undermine our free will. As a result, it's harder to prepare for the future or be truly present in the moment. Instead, we are constantly stuck in the media loop presented to us through our smartphones. It feels like stagnation. And the icing on the top is the overwhelming sensory bombardment of choice and convenience that causes us to atrophy physically, financially, and even environmentally.

The question we are left with is: who are we as a result of this phenomenon? In some regards, we have become less able to make decisions, deprived of awareness of our own misery, and less capable of changing it because tech has made everything so convenient. Welcome to the year 2020, where teenagers are seemingly more depressed than ever and the average American spends twelve or more hours consuming media every day.

In today's attention economy, companies no longer just compete for us as customers or employees—they also compete for us as the product itself. What matters is not how much money you have but how much attention or time you can give up so that tech, and more specifically social media companies, can mold you into a more perfect product.

Companies compete as much for your mind as they do your pocket. Maybe that is why Gen Z's attention span is the shortest of all generations, because it gets pulled into so many directions at the same time. It seems that we are selling our minds cheaply right now—often for free. If we were giving away our dollars like we hand out our attention, we would be pretty poor. So now we have to care about more than just our financial, physical, and relationship health—tech companies are forcing us to take a deep look at our emotional and mental well-being, too.

But not all is bleak. Here is a more optimistic view on the youngest generation. What if Gen Z's short attention span was a positive development? What if it was a defense mechanism developed by their generation to protect their emotional and mental well-being online? What if they can cut to the chase of online content more quickly, preventing themselves from being taken over by it?

There might be some data supporting this belief. Gen Z is less likely to fall for misinformation and fake news, although they consume more news from online sources than any other generation. Could we even say that Gen Z is seven times less likely than boomers to fall for fake content online because they spend more time online, which helps them develop a better grasp of the digital world?[77]

According to a 2018 Pew Research Center survey, 95 percent of thirteen- to seventeen-year-olds have access to a smartphone, and 45 percent of them claim to be online almost constantly.[78] Rather than being a negative, maybe Gen Z's short attention span is actually a positive mental upgrade that helps them stay sane online.

I believe that there is more hope now than ever that we will actually be able to transform ourselves into better-functioning humans through technology. There are many traps on this way, though! Smartphones give companies direct access to your attention. Knowing that should make you question the incentives behind the content you are consuming online.

And these traps lie not only in the external world. They are not only part of the macro changes I described in part I of this book. They also hide within us and can hinder us from reaching our fullest potential, especially in a world that is increasingly capitalizing on our weaknesses.

We've done a deep dive into the external world and discovered some alarming and fascinating trends caused by a shift from living mostly in the physical world to spending most of our waking hours consuming media through digital sources. These trends have caused the outside world to become more complex and less controllable. It has become harder to understand the incentives behind content creation, and that content has thus become less trustworthy. A new currency—our attention—has become the target metric for many companies, especially high-tech firms.

We live in an uncertain, beyond-truth, attention-consuming economy. And while there are some brilliant minds identifying solutions and working with government officials and tech leaders to improve our digital existence, change won't be instant. Even if it did happen quickly, who could guarantee that bad actors wouldn't continue to create fake articles or try to monetize our weaknesses, bad habits, and instant gratification impulses? I believe that bad actors will always be a factor, with or without more regulation.

The solution to this attention-consuming economy lies within us at least as much as it does outside. Let's turn our attention to what we can do inside ourselves and how we can grow into the humans we want to be, so that technology again becomes a source of empowerment instead of a potent tool of manipulation against us. Let's talk about how to understand and adjust the personal "coding" and belief systems that guide our everyday actions, so we can upgrade the relationship we have with ourselves and our technologies.

II

Mindset Upgrades

Congratulations! You've just taken the first step toward a healthier relationship with tech by understanding the external forces that set many of your boundaries, rules, and opportunities. To some degree, we've mapped out what drives the modern world we live in. Just like the relationships you have with your friends, parents, and romantic partner, understanding others and the circumstances that surround them is an essential step to a deeper connection.

So we had to start by uncovering the macro trends that shape us and our digital devices. I believe that it is crucial to understand and accept these forces and limitations before we can work with them or break through them.

But to achieve a breakthrough in our relationship with our smartphones, we need more than just an understanding of those external forces. As a next step, we need to look at our own inner programming. You might be wondering why. Isn't this book about changing the settings on our devices so we feel less hooked? The truth is, that would only get you partway to living an untethered life. You won't turn your phone into a powerful and loyal partner rather than a device of distraction, novelty, and pain avoidance by changing your device settings alone.

This book is meant to support you in becoming an untethered and upgraded version of yourself, someone who can take advantage of the powers available through your devices without feeling dependent on them. And this depends on your inner programming as much as how you set up those devices.

Just like our smartphones, we operate according to our internal programming. It defines how we react to our thoughts and to the information we receive from the outside world. The two together, external input and internal processing, make up who we are and appear to be to others. Which one has a bigger influence on us, I do not know for sure, but I sometimes tell my friends half jokingly that who I am today is 80 percent the influence of my parents, friends, partners, and environment rather than my own true self. So naturally, my goal has become to grow the remaining 20 percent, my own reactions to external stimuli, continuously for the rest of my life.

If we assume for just a second that most of our behaviors and belief systems are highly influenced by our surroundings, we can take two actions to make sure that the influence is as positive as possible. First, as much as possible, we need to surround ourselves with the right people. We all know that some people are more supportive, want to help us succeed and grow, and are more aligned with our own values. The same is true for the places we live and the companies we work for, though I also recognize that making changes in these areas can require a significant financial and personal investment that may be difficult or impossible for some people.

Second, we can reduce potential negative environmental effects by understanding and developing our inner world. Understanding and upgrading our mindset will help us create a baseline ability to cope with the complex, fast paced, uncontrollable external world. It is thus the foundational step in developing your own well-being.

Another advantage of giving attention to our inner world, our reactions and belief systems, is that they are within our control. Although that world is as complex as, and maybe even more complex than, the external world, you are the chief of command in it. And if you feel like you are not in control of your inner world, the good news is you can be if you so desire. In the next five chapters, I will lay out what I believe are the most important beliefs that set you up for success in reconnecting to yourself and finding more fulfillment.

If your feelings of self-worth depend on the external world, you will feel taken advantage of often. You will think that the world is not fair. If you give up your power to somebody else, you will feel disempowered. And if you look for your purpose in the external world, you will often feel disappointed by the paths others have created for you. But how you look at the external world and what you see in it depends on how you program your inner world. And as the commander-in-chief of yourself, you can upgrade that programming.

If we don't update our coding, then rest assured that internet companies have already developed powerful codes of their own for us. Unfortunately, their code has been built with these companies' priorities in mind and thus could easily have downside effects on our well-being. For example, a 2020 Singaporean study on Instagram found that more frequent Instagram use was associated with higher levels of social comparison, which was found to increase social anxiety and decrease levels of self-esteem.[79] If we don't upgrade our own minds, our tech might just continue to downgrade them.

So the power of our inner programming is revealed to us every single day. The way you react to conflict, the number of times you have negative vs. positive thoughts, and your awareness of the influence your words and actions have on others all depend on your programming. Your inner coding does not only change you; it changes how you see the external world. This is scientifically proven in many ways, one of which is called the Baader–Meinhof phenomenon.

Baader–Meinhof is a frequency bias that occurs when your awareness of something increases, leading you to believe that thing is happening more often—even if it's not the case. It's sometimes known as "red car syndrome," a way of explaining why you see more cars of a certain color after buying one yourself. Your brain simply decides to refocus its attention on something new and filter out information that doesn't seem to serve it. And it does this every day. By focusing on some bits of information and ignoring others, your brain creates the reality you perceive. Wouldn't it be nice if you truly loved that reality?

The external and internal worlds balance each other like yin and yang. They are distinctly different from each other, and both have their advantages and disadvantages, but balance between the two is crucial to functioning well. You have to understand the external world to be able to operate within its rules or break them when it's warranted. It's your playing field, but you should never draw your power entirely from it. The inner world is where your power to play comes from. It's a world you are in full control of, even though social media, tech giants, and society often might want you to believe differently.

In the following chapters, I'll talk about mindset upgrades that can jump-start the change you want to see in yourself, positively influence the reality your brain creates for you every day, and increase your readiness for the digital world.

In **Upgrade #1**, we will discuss the cause of some of your misery and the role technology plays in it through the lens of a simple formula. With the help of it, you will be able to reduce some of the negativity in your mind and feel less driven to overuse your tech. Every misery serves a purpose, and recognizing this fact is the start of eliminating it.

Upgrade #2 identifies the powerful role of responsibility and curiosity in creating an untethered life, and how blame and regret can hold you back.

In **Upgrade #3**, we will talk about the most important inspiration for most humans: our purpose in life. I think I've identified a simple but effective way to understand why we are here and how we are supposed to live.

In **Upgrade #4**—my favorite one—I talk about the idea of seeing yourself as three different humans at the same time: Past You, Current You, and the under-represented Future You. This chapter is crucial not only because I believe most of us get stuck in one of those personalities, but also because I believe that technology prefers to interact mostly with one of them. This chapter is also the basis for part III of the book, where you'll learn how to become a fulfilled and untethered version of yourself.

Before we dive in, remember, nobody can walk your journey for you; you alone have the power to take the first steps and become the person you want to be. The following personal upgrades will help you move from smartphone dependency to fulfillment and a balanced relationship with your technology.

UPGRADE #1: TACKLING THE TRUE SOURCE OF NEGATIVITY

"Fighting against your desires doesn't make you more spiritual. Only more frustrated. Desire is natural, yet when it's out of balance, it can become the source of judgment, guilt, depression and addictive behavior."

- **Deepak Chopra**

At this point, it shouldn't be surprising that tech companies strive to capture our attention and sell it to fill their pockets. In the end, we live in a capitalistic society in which we should expect companies to maximize their profits rather than our well-being. Tech companies have done that by capturing our scarcest and most valuable resource: our time. And they have done it so well that most of us will spend more of our time with the black mirrors that surround our lives than we will consciously with friends, family, or partners.

Waking up to this reality is the first step. And I hope the first part of this book helped shine light on how our attention and free will are being manipulated. But understanding the external causes of our tech-centricity is only the start. It's not enough to just know that it is happening—we have to deeply feel that the way things are is not okay! Too often I've asked myself, do I really need to change? Like, how bad is this smartphone dependency, really? Most of the time it feels like I'm just using tech to engage with friends more deeply and enjoy a richer life. Is this truly hurting me that much? Will another hour of Netflix really make a difference?

Before I started my research into tech usage, I didn't think it was too bad. Watching Netflix, browsing the internet, or playing a mobile game just a little longer shouldn't have long-term consequences, right? That's what I thought for quite a while.

Digital technology is without a doubt the most powerful and enriching tool we have ever created. It connects humanity and offers opportunities where none existed before. The complexity it has added to our lives has made them richer. But at the same time, the internet and consumer electronics have transcended from mere tools to agents of addictive habits and misery. We are collectively experiencing how addictions feel, all at the same time. And we are rationalizing our experience.

Who or What Causes Much of Our Suffering?

I think, if asked, most of us would agree that everybody wants to live a happy life on some level, and that seeking happiness drives us. Science, however, has shown that the desire to avoid misery—not the pursuit of happiness—is often what drives our actions.

Misery scares us more than happiness makes us happy. Depression, sadness, and addiction all are results of some kind of misery. Pain avoidance is of even higher priority to us than pure joy-seeking. For example, most people think they will regret foolish actions more than they will regret not having taken risks— and according to studies, they're likely to be wrong in believing this. In hindsight, people complain more regularly and feel more negatively toward their inaction than they do their foolish actions, as Daniel Gilbert describes in Stumbling on Happiness.

So if we're trying that hard to avoid suffering, why do scientific studies show that more than 80 percent of our daily thoughts are negative?[80] That sounds pretty miserable to me! Eighty percent is much more than just a slight bias toward the negative. Our minds seem to create some of our suffering naturally. Sometimes I wonder if we are programmed to be miserable.

One of my favorite meditation teachers, S.N. Goenka, whom you will hear more about later in this book, describes the nature of this negative bias as a cycle of craving and aversion. "You wish to be free from suffering, and instead, you have developed the habit of reacting with craving and clinging to pleasant sensations and with aversion to unpleasant sensations. This habit pattern continues day and night. Even when you are in deep sleep and a sensation arises in the body-if it is unpleasant, you react with aversion; if it is pleasant, you react with craving. This continues all the time for twenty-four hours."[81]

In short, much of our misery might come from us either wanting more of something or trying to avoid something else. We are easily dissatisfied either way. We induce a little suffering every day through our negative bias. Not all suffering is self-created and cannot necessarily be eliminated using tools or techniques like meditation, but the proportion of one's misery that is mostly self-inflicted is addressable.

Mihaly Csikszentmihalyi, a famous psychologist, author, and architect of the notion of "flow," suggests that our brain naturally returns to a state of worry. Clifford Nass, a former professor at Stanford and renowned authority on human–computer interaction, has argued that we have a tendency to see people who say something negative as smarter.

With such a strong bias toward negativity, it seems obvious that relying on our thoughts as a guide can be misleading. With all that negativity, one could claim that our mind has a bias toward causing some of our misery.[82] The self-inflicted negative emotions don't just randomly appear. We have harnessed and fed them for years.

If our minds truly seek out negativity, it makes sense that we use technology to get what we desire. Our devices make it easy for us to feed these cravings and intensify them.

Out of this understanding arise two immediate solutions: we can look at the source of this negativity (our minds), or we can remove the devices that support all of our needs. It seems logical to me to look at ourselves first.

Also, obviously, I have no intention of comparing myself with teachers like Goenka or other spiritual guides. Their knowledge is based on decades of experience and study in the matters of life philosophies and associated life challenges. But what I do want to share and talk about are mindset upgrades as they relate to our use of technology.

I know that I—and probably many others—tend to quickly seek out blame when something doesn't work in my life. I blamed my phone for the time it was "taking" from me before realizing that I was, at least to some degree, creating this miserable situation. I did that on one hand because my smartphone was readily available and wouldn't say anything back when being blamed. But there was another element that became clear after years of negativity toward my smartphone.

I think that a lot of my own misery and dissatisfaction in life was explainable with one simple equation.

If E > R then D else H

A lot of Dissatisfaction (D) in my life occurs when I do not meet my past expectations (E at T-1) in today's reality (R at time T). Said differently, when my past expectations for the future are greater than what the future turns out to be, I become disappointed with myself. Sadness, depression, avoidance, and many other symptoms can be the consequence of that dissatisfaction. But when expectations are lower and reality is better than we'd imagined, then we can expect happiness.

Obviously, we don't experience reality in such a black-and-white way. Dissatisfaction and happiness coexist in most of us. But if we look at our experiences at a granular level, this formula makes a lot of sense.

A lot of my dissatisfactions come from not doing what I'd planned to do, not having what I'd planned to have, or not achieving what I'd imagined I would. Basically, when my expectations or plans don't meet reality, I become unsatisfied.

Humans are uniquely capable of planning or imagining our futures—and becoming unhappy through unmet expectations. The frontal lobe of our brain is responsible for projecting ourselves into potential future scenarios and then evaluating what those experiences might be like. This part of the brain helps us determine if it makes sense for us to take certain risks with the hope of a specific outcome.

You could even call this the most unique feature of the human species. Alfred North Whitehead, a famous English mathematician and philosopher, said in the late 1800s that "the purpose of thinking is to let the ideas die instead of us dying." He was referring to the tremendous task of the frontal lobe to put ourselves in our future shoes and evaluate how something could go right or wrong in order to make a decision about whether to put our real selves on that path.

Our ability to imagine and expect what the future might be like and then prepare for it is an extremely useful survival mechanism. But having expectations also comes with the disadvantage that we have to deal with the emotional consequences when some of them don't come to fruition. The future is inherently uncertain, and our understanding of it will always be limited, and thus we will often fail to achieve our own expectations.

We have all experienced this in some fashion: a friend joining you an hour late to a dinner, your partner not buying the groceries they promised to get, or your boss handing you an unexpectedly negative performance review. We all experience disappointment, and we all understand what it feels like. Some of us are capable of shrugging it off quickly, but others carry it with them for days, weeks, months, and even years.

Disappointments are difficult to deal with at any level, but are particularly devastating when they arise from our life goals. At some point in our life we all ask ourselves this same question, consciously or not: "Am I doing now what I want to and planned to in the past?" The answer is often no.

It happened to me as early as high school. I felt disempowered because I felt forced to be there. I had other goals than sitting in class: more time outside playing sports, getting fitter, making deeper connections with friends, finding the partner of my dreams, starting my own business, getting into a great college, and simply eating healthier.

One of my most painful experiences where reality did not meet my expectations happened while dating. I was single for many years, between 2010 and 2017. Until 2015, dating was fun, easy, and mostly successful, with only small setbacks. This felt great, but it also meant I wasn't prepared for failure. At the end of 2015, I fell in love with somebody who didn't feel the same way. Because of my past success with dating, I had already anticipated what our future would be like. I was certain of it. My expectations were high, but they were never even close to met.

Even worse, for two years on and off, the other person would give me hope that my expectations might one day be met. I woke up thinking about her most mornings. It was painful and distracting. The experience overloaded my human CPU with background tasks (or thoughts, as we call them): *Should I write her now or later? What should I say? Is this silly? What would she like me to do? How can I get her to come to this event with me?*

I was trapped in a loop that constantly took me out of the present moment. My brain was creating a dark reality that existed only for me, one in which I was constantly disappointed by myself. I sought relief through my smartphone and more dating, to try to meet some of my desires to be in control and loved. But it wasn't until I accepted that I was the cause of a lot of my misery that things started to shift slowly.

Do you remember a moment when you sought escape through your smartphone and ended up causing more harm? Do you ever remember setting a goal for the day but then spending most of it with your devices instead of making real progress? How did you feel after? Most of us have experienced waking up feeling energized and ready to pursue our goals... then we unlock our phones.

Messages await, and we see invitations to events or notifications to engage with content, like watching a YouTube video or reading an article. Before you know it, we've gone from energized and goal oriented to confused and anxious. And then instead of focusing on what matters, we feel overwhelmed by the choices and give in to whatever our phone presents to us in the most enticing way. The day flies by, and by the end we are left with unmet expectations and unachieved goals—with disappointment, anger, and frustration directed at either ourselves or our device.

Our devices are built to give us many great options to work and play, and they are also built to draw us in. But we are still responsible for choosing what is right for us. Unfortunately, we often increase our suffering through our unconscious tech habits.

In general, when we become aware of our goals and desires, we often feel either disappointed about failing to achieve them or super ready to take the steps to achieve what we envision. We feel like someone who signed up at Planet Fitness in the first week of January after planning their new fitness regimen over the winter break. We're ready to do it!

But just like a newly motivated gym member, as time passes, our motivations for having a summer body fade. By March, life just gets too busy, and we cancel the gym membership. Disappointment kicks in, followed by an attempt to rationalize it away. "I'm too busy at work." "Exam season is about to start, and I really need to focus." Whatever the excuse, it just masks the underlying disappointment over not following through and achieving our dreams.

Our digital devices make it easier than ever to be distracted from our life goals and expectations. We can avoid looking at our own failures by escaping into technology, but in a conscious moment our present self remembers some of the dreams and desires of the past version of itself. And when that happens, we can decide to either find relief in our black mirrors, or tackle that misery head-on.

The great (and kind of sad) news is that humans are incredibly capable of avoiding their misery for long periods of time—and our devices make it even easier. But at some point, not looking at our dreams or understanding that we are self-inflicting some of our suffering will haunt us. Creating an untethered life requires us to accept our misery and our role in causing it; otherwise, we will continue to seek relief in the digital world.

Healthy Ways to Tackle Expectations and Negativity

First, and most obviously, we can work on lowering our expectations to avoid the perception of failure. And there is evidence that this might actually be possible.

Some people have shown that through a lifetime of dedicated effort, it may be possible to achieve a state of well-being without expectations. Dr. Jeffrey Martin (whom I will talk more about in Upgrade #4) has studied people who experience what he calls "fundamental well-being." One of their common traits is that they have fewer thoughts about the future; some even have a hard time imagining themselves in future scenarios. They also experience fewer negative thoughts and expectations.

Unfortunately, the path to becoming one of those people is not yet very clear—it likely involves luck, biological disposition, or uncommonly constructive reactions to certain life experiences. Lifelong meditators can also achieve similar states.

Another, maybe easier solution comes from revisiting our formula. What if we could adjust that formula in our favor and reduce the weight our expectations carry?

Old: If E > R then D else H

NEW: If (wxE) > R then D else H

What if instead of being disappointed by not achieving something, we could receive that information with less suffering? If we could just apply a coefficient to the formula above to reduce the weight (w) our expectations carry, we could experience happiness even when we don't fully meet our expectations. But how can we lower the weight to maybe 0.5 instead of multiplying our misery by being so set on achieving our expectations?

I know it might sound a little unrealistic, but I promise you that in part III, we will be looking at some tools that can help us increase our awareness of our own expectations and how we are creating them. Awareness is the key to taking control and reducing our desire to distract ourselves from the misery of unmet expectations with unhealthy technology habits.

This path is possible. We have access to more opportunities today than ever before. But we are also more distracted than ever. Our smartphones have become the gatekeepers of our attention and desires. Because the companies that service the black mirrors in our lives all have one goal in mind: satisfy our current needs so that we spend more time and money with them. They love to keep meeting our immediate needs, but they don't pay attention to our long-term desires.

The digital world is designed to distract us and keep us engaged in ways we don't benefit from. Unfortunately, we can't wait around for the system to self-regulate. We can, however, empower ourselves to create the change we want to see in the world.

Our unhealthy relationship with our smartphones is not our fault, but it is our responsibility to improve it.

Instead of focusing all of our frustration on "the system" or the companies that have turned our attention into a commodity, we can regain our power by taking responsibility for that attention and working to understand the ways we might be self-inflicting misery.

This path requires listening to ourselves deeply. It requires exploring different ways of living until we find alignment. And most of all, it requires taking responsibility for the misery we create for ourselves instead of blaming our devices for it.

As you already know, the average American spends over twelve hours a day consuming media. That's twelve hours filled with opportunities to avoid looking at our shadows, problems, and desires. Unfortunately, our desire to escape makes sense in the bigger context. Depression rates have been rising for years now—especially among young adults—and while the world has become a better place by some metrics, negative sentiment has been increasing. American productivity has increased significantly, but pay has not, nor have happiness levels. Plus a pandemic has literally cut us off from each other. There are endless reasons to seek escape.

We have the most powerful devices ever created in our hands, machines that enable distraction and escapism in the short term but ultimately cause disappointment when used predominantly for those reasons. For most of us, our brains create a perception of the world that is negatively biased, which nudges us into using our phones more frequently to escape into the digital world. The process of healing our relationship with our devices requires that we understand ourselves, how we self-inflict misery, and how we can better manage our expectations.

Upgrade #1: Understand and accept that your brain self-inflicts negativity, that we can be attached to it and that you have the power to change some of it by understanding and managing your expectations.

UPGRADE #2: COMMITTING TO RESPONSIBILITY, CURIOSITY AND YOUR POWERS

"In the long run, people of every age and in every walk of life seem to regret not having done things much more than they regret things they did."

- **Dan Gilbert**

In 2019 and 2020, I was helping a small startup in Berkeley with their marketing and product strategy. It was one of my favorite gigs during those two years. The founders were a hard-working team of three friends—I'll call them Peter, Amar, and Tony—who were deeply committed to each other and their vision. Like so many aspiring founders, they had moved together to Silicon Valley in 2018 to change the world according to their vision.

The three had been friends since middle school and their friendship seemed unbreakable. Together, they decided to leave their home country and move abroad to work together on a startup, spending ten, twelve, sometimes fourteen hours a day, six days a week to make their dreams come true. They lived and worked together, basically spending every hour of their waking lives with each other. Although this constant proximity would have driven many people nuts, they seemed to thoroughly enjoy it.

At the beginning of my engagement, I couldn't predict how their relationship would end, but I was suspicious about the viability of spending that much time with each other.

The first cracks in their three-way relationship became apparent at the end of 2019 when Tony decided to move back home. Tony's wife was back home waiting to start a family, and wanted Tony to come home. She gave him an ultimatum, and Tony gave in.

But he did not do so without committing to help the team until they'd found somebody to replace him. He agreed to stay with the company for another six months, and accepted a reduction in his stock package. Tony's willingness to prolong his engagement and give up stock seemed like a strong sign of friendship and commitment to help the company succeed.

But at the beginning of 2020, I noticed their relationship started to change. Although they had just moved into a beautiful new home with a stunning view of San Francisco, raised a round of funding, and attracted some great talent, the company's future was less certain with Tony exiting. And Amar was handling it poorly.

In January, Amar moved out of their house into an apartment. He started to dissociate himself from the achievements and failures of their startup, and even from his own successes and failures. He began blaming others more and taking less responsibility for his work. He was becoming more fearful, less committed, and less trusting.

These changes weren't very noticeable at first because Amar rarely spoke about his feelings. Nonetheless, he was unable to fully hide his disapproval of Tony's departure, and regularly blamed Tony for no longer being able to commit to the company long term.

By February, Amar's behavioral changes had become obvious to their employees as well. He was easily upset by seemingly small issues, and even left several meetings angrily. Amar stopped taking responsibility and instead doubled down on blaming his friends, mostly Peter, the company's CEO. His curiosity and desire to solve problems was replaced with a need to be right.

While I believe Amar when he says that some of the behaviors toward him by the other founders were unacceptable, I do not believe that he truly tried solving those issues. Instead, he let blame and righteousness take over.

In early March, the company let go of Amar, after two months full of blame, bitterness, anger, and demoralization. I believe that there is a good chance that Peter and Tony won't talk to Amar for many years to come. So how did Peter, Amar, and Tony go from childhood friends, roommates, and business partners to enemies in only a few months?

When things don't go the way we think they should, our natural reaction is to become anxious and fearful. With fear often comes blaming and taking on the victim role. In the book *The 15 Commitments of Conscious Leaders*, Jim Dethmer, Diana Chapman, and Kaley Klemp describe the blame pattern that keeps us stuck as having four stages:

1. Something doesn't go the way we think it should.

2. We become stuck in fear (which often manifests as anger).

3. We blame others, ourselves, or the system.

4. Relationships solidify around the roles of victim, villain, and hero.

I refer to this as the "blame death spiral." No matter whether you are child-hood friends, business partners, or roommates (or all three at once), the blame death spiral is a mortal enemy to any relationship. Nobody can win, and every-body loses. The side effects of the death spiral are anger, bitterness, resentment, demotivation, inability to see growth opportunities, and a demoralized sense that nothing will ever change. The spiral, if reinforced for long enough, will end any otherwise functioning relationship... with your partner, your family, your tech devices, and even yourself!

The first commitment in *The 15 Commitments of Conscious Leaders* describes taking personal responsibility for the circumstances of one's life as the antidote to blaming. I would go so far as to say that it is the basis to living a fulfilled life.

Let me explain with an example. Buying a house is a major life goal for most Americans. Living in a house gives a feeling of physical comfort and allows us to express our individuality, among many other upsides compared to living on the streets. We can easily grasp the importance of having ownership over our physical space. We don't want to allow others to decide where and how we should live, and buying a home gives us long-term autonomy and control over our daily living experience.

But while our physical space might be very much in our control, we too often decide to hand over control of our mental space to somebody else through the blame death spiral. Within the framework of the blame death spiral, things are being done "to us" that we often don't agree with. We are at the will of somebody else who can take us anywhere they want. Whenever we allow our lives to fall apart because of something somebody did "to us," we are consciously or uncon-sciously choosing to do that.

So why do we give in to the blame death spiral and cede ownership of our mental well-being so often? Because the alternative—taking full responsibility—means taking ownership of mistakes or bad outcomes. It can feel like an attack on our ego, and even on our self-worth and our understanding of who we are.

Being radically responsible for yourself—for your attention and your well-being—is a prerequisite to living a fulfilled and untethered life.

Even once you recognize that you are self-inflicting harm, you may still find yourself blaming others occasionally. But if you are conscious of it, and can quickly take back control and responsibility for your actions, you are on a solid path to living with a greater sense of fulfillment.

Self-responsibility also means taking back control and opening up space to grow. Growth is sometimes painful if attachment to the old self is too strong. Can you accept that the You of yesterday is not the You of today? Can you accept that growth is probably the best way to sustain who you are in a world that is so rapidly changing?

Our devices often prevent us from stepping into self-responsibility. Avoiding our issues was pretty easy even before Twitch, social media, or online games, but now it is only one hand motion away. The conveniences provided by digital technologies make it easier than ever to avoid looking at ourselves or taking responsibility for how we spend our time.

I am not saying this to blame you or anybody else. I am not trying to call you out. I still seek escape through my devices more often than I would like to admit. But the reality is that deep down, most of us know that we are doing it.

So how do we start this radical self-responsibility? It would be great if we could just flip a switch and start living every minute feeling aligned with our purpose. But honestly, in this case, I have a secret cheat code to become more responsible immediately.

Invest in Your Curiosity

Curiosity can lead to radical self-responsibility. It is as simple as asking yourself a question every time you notice yourself doing something unexpected. Whether that is making a mistake or simply having an amazing day, when I realize that something out of the ordinary is happening, I let curiosity guide me and I ask myself: "I notice something was just different. What happened?"

This little trick allows me to be more curious about my own behaviors, understand myself and other people better, and take more responsibility for my actions. And by the way, when I catch myself watching YouTube for a long time, I ask the exact same question. "I notice something was just different. What happened"? Posing that question frequently has made me realize that I often use YouTube when I unconsciously desire to procrastinate over difficult or less exciting work.

Curiosity opens new perspectives, and when paired with self-responsibility it makes us less tethered. Without curiosity, we think we already know what's best for us, which opens the door to biases, misinformation, and misconceptions. It becomes harder to make informed decisions.

Upgrading your mind to enable curiosity is another requirement of an untethered life. Without it, you are likely to continue engaging in unhealthy digital habits without ever asking what purpose they might be serving. Commit to taking radical responsibility for your life and to being curious over being right. Righteousness must be constantly defended, while curiosity needs only to be fed. And curiosity becomes easier and easier once you get the hang of it! No need to waste your energy on defense; use it to fuel the curious exploration that will allow you to grow.

Take the example of Amar. He decided to blame his best friend, who was taking responsibility for his own life by making a difficult decision. Amar could have acted through curiosity, which would have likely deepened their friendship. Instead of trying to understand, he decided to condemn his friend for allegedly abandoning him and the team. Amar's decision to continue down the blame death spiral cost him a great friendship and possibly much more.

But don't just take my word for it. Curiosity comes with scientifically proven benefits. According to different studies, curiosity primes the brain for learning,[83] it positively influences the depth of connection you make with others,[84] and it increases life satisfaction and happiness.[85] It just makes so much sense to use this little trick to become more self-responsible.

Here are some other ways that you can enable curiosity in your life, none of which require your smartphone:

1. Be curious about friends. In situations with your friends, aim to ask at least one question that you feel deeply curious about. One question that would make you understand them better.

2. Be curious about life. Try to do one thing every week you've never done before.

3. Be curious about the people around you. Talk to at least one stranger every week.

It is this simple to start being a little more curious!

You might be wondering, how will talking to a stranger every week help me untether? Well, the more you grow accustomed to having new experiences regularly, the more opportunities you have to ask yourself: What was different about that? How could I do that differently in the future? What did I learn from that experience? Whether you're asking these questions about trying a new food or having an argument with a friend, you are practicing the art of being curious rather than being right. You will feel less blame and anger and feel more empowered to make better choices for next time.

This includes how you interact with your smartphone. Rather than feeling anger and blame when you emerge from a one-hour Instagram or Youtube bender, ask yourself: What thoughts was I having that I was trying to avoid? What feelings was I trying to avoid? Get curious about yourself rather than clinging to shame or frustration. Practice looking at yourself with curiosity instead of judgement.

The story of Amar has one more lesson to teach us. Whenever possible, try to preserve important relationships by avoiding the blame death spiral, and be aware of those around you who seem to need to always be right. (I am sure you know people with that mindset!) Curiosity and responsibility are the baseline requirement to keeping and fostering relationships with others—and especially with yourself. They are prerequisites for staying on the path toward an untethered life.

Believe me, there is no worse feeling than knowing in hindsight that bad outcomes could have been avoided by simply shifting into curiosity and responsibility. Amar could have remained an executive at his startup and had an even better relationship with his business partners and friends if he had stayed curious and taken responsibility for his actions. And the same applies to our daily use of technology. We have the power to achieve our dreams by utilizing tech in healthy ways, but it requires lots of responsibility to use those powerful machines to address our needs and not the tech companies'.

"The people who don't ask questions remain clueless throughout their lives."

- **Neil DeGrasse Tyson**

Be Courageous

One of my favorite movies of all time is 2017's *King Arthur: Legend of the Sword*. It's probably not the highest rated movie you'll ever watch, but I've seen it many times. I may have even forced my family and friends to watch it too.

At the beginning of his journey, King Arthur is not the noble hero you might expect. He's more like a local Robin Hood: a bad guy in the eyes of the law, but someone with a good heart who's attempting to take ownership of his life and improve the lives of the people around him. He collects gold and silver coins to get himself and his friends out of poverty, but makes a mistake one day that turns his orderly and simple life into total chaos. He loses everything—his possessions, freedom, and friends—and as a result starts the journey of discovering himself, of finding his truth.

During that journey, he comes across Excalibur, a sword only he can use, one that magnifies his powers. Excalibur represents Arthur's potential, his unique gift and ability to mold chaos into the order he envisions. But he doesn't know that at first. In the movie, there are several scenes in which the soon-to-be king places his hands on Excalibur and enters a dream-like, visionary state in which he sees himself fulfilling his deepest potential. He learns that his super power of caring for others in combination with Excalibur allows him to slow time and bend the world to his will. Every time he touches the sword, it presents him with his own potential.

But the surprising part is the way he handles uncovering his potential. First, he faints after Excalibur unveils his tremendous abilities. He drops the sword or simply walks away from it. He is scared to take on the responsibility of power. At one point, one of the other heroes in the story looks at him after he releases the sword and tells him, "It is okay, we all look away."

It was at that moment that I realized the power of this story for each one of us. This movie—in my interpretation—is not about beautiful animation, well-executed fight scenes, or funny dialogue. Underneath all that, King Arthur is a story about the bravery it requires to look at ourselves truly and deeply, and to then accept the possibilities that lie within us.

I believe the hard part is not in finding your passions or your powers. It is accepting it within you even once you know it. Very few doubted King Arthur's potential; the biggest doubter was himself. Understanding how difficult the path ahead is once we commit to our powers is frightening. We can change the world, but can we handle the responsibility that comes with it?

And this is what Arthur realizes every time he grips the sword tightly: his path, the power he has to create a world more aligned with his wishes, the pain and suffering that will be part of this path, and finally, the responsibility he will carry for himself and many others.

The great thing about the King Arthur story is that we all know the ending. Arthur accepts the sword and chooses to live up to his fullest potential, or at least attempts to do so every day. Can we do the same in our own lives?

Joseph Campbell calls this type of story the "hero's journey." Born in 1904, Campbell spent much of his life comparing religions and mythology across different cultures. In this work, he started noticing patterns and similarities between these stories and their characters. He figured it was impossible for most of these cultures to have interacted with each other or shared their stories extensively with each other. The internet was not a thing, nor did most people speak more than a single language.

These stories have often been passed from one generation to the next and have shaped the human psyche. But Campbell discovered that most of them have an underlying narrative and follow the same structure: the hero's journey.

The journey starts with a call for adventure. The hero hears the call, but at first they're reluctant. They ignore and refuse to give in. Then, something in the hero's life pushes them over the edge and into the adventure. Along the way, the hero experiences hardship, encounters enemies, and gets help from friends and strangers. There is a moment where the hero is confronted with the thing they wanted, but it becomes clear that the desired thing is different than expected. The hero makes a decision, and is changed by it. They take a new role and come back to their home with the prize to integrate into the world.

Campbell argues that deep down, we all create this same story arc in our lives—only in real life, we never know if we will rise up to the challenge. Few people make a conscious effort to tap into their full potential. And that is part of the tragedy of life. And it is this unfulfilled potential that will haunt us. Don't take my word for it—take Bronnie Ware's.

Bronnie wrote the book *The Top Five Regrets of Dying*. She spent several years caring for patients during the last few months of their lives, routinely asking her patients if they had regrets or thoughts about how they would have lived their lives differently. Among other things, she discovered that we rarely show gratitude for what we've achieved but rather remorse for the things we've knowingly let slip through our hands—especially the things we know would have been in alignment with our deepest selves, with our potential.[86]

To avoid this regret, you must figure out and embrace your potential, even if the prospect of accepting your powers feels paralyzing. Our minds are drawn to negativity, so they tend to present us with negative prospects. When your prefrontal lobe helps you imagine all the future misery, all the hardship, all the pushbacks you will encounter on your path, you might think, why should I even attempt this journey? Wouldn't it be more comfortable to just live my normal life and leave my potential unfulfilled? Yes, it would—and most people will make that decision, consciously or not.

> "Most people think they will regret foolish actions more than foolish inactions. But studies have shown that 9 out of 10 people are wrong."
>
> - **Daniel Gilbert,** Stumbling on Happiness

In the long run, people regret the things they didn't do more than the things they did. The studies are clear on that. Our brains are more capable of rationalizing courage than cowardice. We regret unfortunate outcomes we could have controlled if we'd chosen differently. But even when we choose the wrong action by doing something new and risky, at least we've tried. And that's what matters and what will help you reduce future regrets. You can't turn back time, so you'd better start living your truest self now. Avoiding regrets probably means taking some (calculated) risks, and chances are you haven't taken enough of them yet.

Bronnie speaks about the clarity that a lot of people gain at the end of their lives and describes the common themes that surfaced during these conversations. I think that these five simple statements are not only major lessons but actually describe, to some degree, how to take self-responsibility:

- I wish I'd had the courage to live a life true to myself, not the life others expected of me.

- I wish I hadn't worked so much.

- I wish I'd had the courage to express my feelings.

- I wish I had stayed in touch with my friends.

- I wish I had let myself be happier.

Put in one simple sentence, it could read something like this: Take care of becoming yourself, work less, express your feelings more, maintain and grow relationships and allow yourself to be happy! A human who can do these well already is extremely powerful. Be courageous enough to be yourself independent of what the world thinks about it.

Our smartphones and other devices can support us on this path by giving us more access to wealth, so that we can work less; to other humans, so that we can express our feelings and grow relationships; and to a new digital world, allowing us to express our happiness in novel ways. But our devices also have the potential to prevent us from embracing our power by enabling distractions that feel good in the moment but have little future value.

What powers do you have that you've kept hidden from the world? Do you find yourself reaching for your phone to get distracted when you imagine your future or are you actually taking responsibility to take directed steps toward it? What are you avoiding and why? How is tech giving you an out, and how could you be more courageous?

Bronnie has learned from many of her clients that to experience the beauty of life fully, you need courage. Courage to live in alignment with your needs and desires. Courage to accept yourself and your powers. Courage is required to accept your powers and the powers of your devices to live a fuller life.

The Consequences of Responsibility

Fortunately, we all have access to arguably the most powerful devices in the world: our smartphones. They can be used as wonderful tools for creation or literally destroy a life. We are lucky to live in times where we can combine the power of our body, mind and soul with the power that we hold in our hands. Accept that you are powerful and so is your smartphone. Power comes with responsibility. If you don't control your power, it will control you. Accept that you have it, be courageous, and know that you can control it.

Also, you might not know this, but you are already well on your way to accepting your power! You have taken the first steps by bringing awareness to the thoughts that create your misery, becoming more self responsible, and by getting back into the curious mindset of a lifelong learner.

When you are miserable, when you continue to make excuses and blame others, you are giving away your power. In doing that you often find relief, just like you do when scrolling through your smartphone. Both can be ways to escape an uncomfortable reality. The way we use this powerful device is just a mere reflection of who we currently are.

If you take away one thing from this chapter, it is that nobody else can take responsibility for you. Nobody else can explore your inner world. And finally, nobody else knows what your true power is. Trust yourself and your own powers. Understand that and know that you will be well on this path if you act with curiosity and courage. Both will enable you to connect more deeply with yourself, deal with the powers that lie in our technologies and, ultimately, take responsibility for your untethered life.

* * *

Next comes Upgrade #3. My favorite part about the next chapter is that it will give you a chance to practice stepping into curiosity right away. It was one of the more vulnerable chapters for me to write because I am attempting to talk about something that many famous and well-read philosophers have been trying to figure out for as long as we are human. I want to speak about the purpose of life—or at least what I perceive it to be.

Before I talk about it, I want to mention that you might not accept or agree with what I say. I understand and respect that fully. My intention with Upgrade #3 is not to suggest you discard your existing beliefs or guiding philosophies. But I do want to help you put your usage of digital technologies in perspective and eliminate some of the complexity that can make you feel overwhelmed.

Upgrade #2: As long as you haven't started taking full responsibility for your actions, you are not in control of your well-being. Commit to your true power by enabling it through curiosity and courage.

UPGRADE #3: UNDERSTANDING OUR PURPOSE

We spent some time understanding the first two mindset changes needed for an untethered relationship with our smartphones. As long as we believe that other people have power over us, as long as we do not commit to the power within us, and as long as we are not truly curious, major changes in our relationship with ourselves and technology won't likely happen.

In this chapter, we will talk about an upgrade that is at the core of life itself—the question of its purpose. I will take a stab at articulating what I believe is a purpose to life derived from biology. You might believe that life has a different purpose altogether, and that's okay. What I am going to explore is the idea of a shared purpose. I believe that a large majority of our tech habits today are working against this purpose and thus cause us pain.

You might disagree with the concept of a shared purpose, but give me a chance to explain. When we envision our future life, we often state all the things we want to have achieved—the countries we want to visit, the money we want to have, the friendships we want to foster, etc. But when we ask ourselves what we truly want from these goals, at the heart of the answer most of the time lies the need to feel happy, fulfilled, and useful. Most of us share these common desires. And we hope to meet them by understanding our life's purpose and living it out fully.

But in my experience, not everybody will find a specific, personal purpose that will make them happy. My friend Adam Smiley Poswolsky interviewed many people who found alternative routes in life and still found happiness without one specific purpose. If you are curious how they did it, he wrote about them in his excellent book, *The Quarter-Life Breakthrough.*

On a personal front, I believe that humans are too multifaceted to just have one clearly defined purpose or desire that drives them. The same person can enjoy driving cars, being a dad, playing with toys, eating ice cream, sleeping long hours, and working hard. It is human to have many different desires, to want to explore. I believe we obsess over finding our purpose so much that we forget about the purpose of living, the meta purpose to life. I catch myself obsessing over finding my true purpose more often than I'd like to admit.

Instead of helping you understand what specific work you are supposed to do on this planet, I want to describe what I believe living beings are here to do in the first place. While our personal life purpose shows up differently for every-body, we are all living creatures bound by the laws of nature. In the end, we're all on similar journeys and have similar desires based on our shared human nature. We all want to know why we're here and what we can give to humanity.

I'm one of those people who hasn't found the "thing" that I thought I was supposed to do. Sometimes I still catch myself secretly hoping to find that one purpose—only to accept that I might not have just one but many. And that is actually beautiful!

My friend Smiley says that today's young adults will have at least seven different jobs throughout their careers. The majority of millennials actually expect to change jobs every 3 years.[87] It's very common to have different passions and changing preferences. Our life's purpose is no longer to find that one passion. I personally never found that one thing. I had glimpses of it, here and there. But there never turned out to be this one personal purpose that I was living this life for. And that's okay. Most of us will not find that one thing.

Our Shared Purpose in the Digital Age

If you think of your genes as the end result of millions of years of experimentation, it is easy to argue that we are perhaps the most complex animal nature has ever created. Humans are billions strong, and most of us are connected through the internet all the time. We make individual decisions and decisions as a species. We can send information across the world within fractions of a second. Humanity rocks, thanks to the incredible genes we carry!

From a biological perspective, each one of us is equipped with an uniquely generated set of genes. Although we share 99.9 percent of our genes with each other, the remainder is what makes every single DNA sequence unique. As we age, differences in gene expression carry out and we become more unique.

By allowing our genes to express themselves in their own unique ways, we are doing humanity a favor. We are basically testing out a new combination of DNA and its ability to make it in this world. Every one of us is a unique experiment in surviving and thriving on this planet. Our DNA is continuously experimenting within the limitations of energy, space, and time, to find its most optimal expression in a given environment.

This genetic purpose finds its highest realization in reproduction. For any species to survive, its members need to mate, to share their string of biological information with another's string (though some species' individuals can reproduce by themselves) to produce offspring that contain a new DNA combination. Reproduction is a way for DNA to expand and test new ways of being within the current environmental limitations. Life's goal is to produce unique DNA experiments to ensure it survives and thrives.

By creating new combinations of DNA strings in an everlasting contest of creation and optimization, life can explore itself more deeply and more uniquely. Life, essentially, is exploring and optimizing itself. If life itself is constantly exploring new ways of being, does that not also mean that the purpose of our individual lives is to explore?

Each one of us is given a unique starting point in life. From there we develop, exploring different ways of being to find the one that best suits us. Unfortunately, many of us get stuck within the expectations of our social circle and never get to fully express or explore our differences. But the only way to find our uniqueness is by exploring what life has to offer to find the ways we are best suited to showcase our subtle differences.

The purpose of life might simply be to explore itself fully. Or at least, this is how I interpret it. Our DNA can only express itself uniquely if we understand all our abilities and limitations. And to some degree, we know and understand that deep down inside. Being an explorer is fun; trying new things gives us joy. Whether we're googling some new piece of information, trying out #vanlife, or just smelling flowers on our way to school or work, exploring life brings joy.

Some of the anecdotal evidence for exploration being so key to fulfillment can be found in the top regrets of dying as described in Upgrade #2. Many people claim on their deathbeds that they wished they'd had the courage to live a life true to themselves, that they hadn't worked so much, that they'd had the courage to express their feelings, and that they'd let themselves be happier. People inherently desire to explore life more and to be less bound by social limitations. Expressing yourself fully is a need that we recognize, but often only when it is too late.

So what happens when the wheels of exploration stop turning? What happens when we stop creating, connecting, building, forming, and socializing? Among other things, we get bored. For example, we get bored when we listen to the same song too much.[88] Research shows that after a certain number of times, we know a song so well that we don't want to hear it for an extended period of time.

And what happens when we get bored? We invite our smartphones in for rescue. While we could use that boredom to meditate, to do sports, just sit with it, or perform any other healthy activity, we instead often get away from that responsibility by drowning ourselves in a black mirror. We see boredom as something that needs to be prevented. Boredom in itself is a sign. A sign that might nudge us to rest or to explore, but one we often mistake instead as a sign to overload our system with content.

But when our brains are constantly stimulated, learning is prevented.[89] Studies show that some major cross-sections of our brains are active during downtime.[90] That means that periods of rest might be needed to work through and store information in our mind.

New research from the Australian National University also argues that boredom can actually spark precious creativity.[91] The study's lead researcher, Guihyun Park, says, "People want to get out of a boring state, so they indulge in novelty-seeking unique thinking." Boredom is the spark that helps us create new, engaging ways of exploring the world. Boredom could essentially be an alarm function that reminds us to explore and be more creative.

Boredom is like nature's kick in the butt—but little did nature know about this thing called a smartphone that absorbs any type of pain momentarily. Can you use your boredom as a driver to seek more engagement with life instead of a signal to become distracted? Can you treat boredom as an indicator that it is time to explore, not as a sign to load up the next YouTube video?

"Emotions are information in need of action."

- **Karla McLaren**, The Art of Empathy

Exploration could include any consciously chosen activity, new or old. It could mean deciding to go to the gym, meditating or giving a compliment to a stranger. Naturally, each one of us should only explore in ways that and as much as our physical, emotional, and mental structure allows us to cope with. Going too far beyond our capabilities will hurt us. Our limits are valid and part of our genetic build up. Always stay true to yourself when exploring.

How to Become More of an Explorer

When we explore, we learn and grow. We become more fully aligned with our true selves and grow our understanding of ourselves. Exploration leads to personal growth. But how do you know for sure that you are developing and exploring? Let me show you a simple framework:

At the end of 2017, my friend Emily sent an invitation and instructions for a "Jeffersonian dinner".[92] Instead of a regular dinner, she organized one with the purpose of growth and exploration. Ten people would be sitting at one table dining together, but only one person would be allowed to talk at any given time. Only one conversation could be had simultaneously at the dinner table—meaning no side conversations or using our smartphones.

When speaking, you had to address the entire table, instead of addressing an individual person directly. The idea was to increase the probability of building shared knowledge through focused discussions on a single topic. It was a rare opportunity to learn from nine other people at the same time.

A few hours into the dinner, someone asked the question, "How do you measure personal development?" I started wondering myself: *How do you measure how much you're exploring and growing?* A couple of us offered answers, but they were incomplete and unsatisfying—until my friend Renee spoke up. She said that her prior employer had defined a way to measure personal development:

"Becoming more comfortable with what was previously uncomfortable."

Being comfortable to me has always meant being lazy. Western society, and my friends and my parents in particular, have taught me that lazy people are bad people. In order to be worthy in society, you have to be productive. In order to survive, you have to create value for others. In school, teachers taught me to be productive, to study hard, and to solve problems by investing time and effort that would give me better grades and, ultimately, a better chance of survival.

Nobody ever told me that comfort was part of the equation of life. So, of course, I was resistant to the idea initially. But then I had an insight: I realized that a state of comfort can also be described as a state of knowing.

Do you remember when you learned to ride a bicycle for the first time? It was probably difficult initially. You might have fallen off several times and even hurt yourself. Maybe you cried; I certainly did. I remember my sister being really really good at it from the start, which was annoying back then. I guess I was jealous, because my learning process was painful and stressful.

But after a few days of practice, you start getting really good at it. You might even start to think that you are a better bicyclist than you actually are—

meaning the feeling of psychological comfort on the bike grows faster than your body's ability to handle the bike. This might lead to an accident or two—small bumps on the road to becoming fully comfortable riding bicycles.

Eventually, though, riding becomes so easy that it gradually takes up less and less of our brain capacity. Slowly, we let go of one hand. Remember how cool you felt the first time you did that? I do. But that milestone wasn't the end to my growing comfort level with riding bicycles. A few months later, I was able to hold something in my hand while riding. God, that felt great. Fast-forward to today, and I could ride my bike while texting on my phone without feeling like I'm overloading my system, though I obviously don't recommend doing that. Bicycling has become extremely comfortable. Not as intuitive as walking, but close to it.

But here's the crazy thing. It used to be extremely common to meet other kids and their parents who didn't know how to ride a bike. Just seventy years ago, half of the world's population was illiterate. Just imagine, 50 percent of people being uncomfortable when presented with written words. Once we become comfortable with something, it becomes second nature. After a while, we can hardly imagine other people being uncomfortable with that same thing.

Being comfortable with something that was previously uncomfortable means that we've learned something, that we've grown and progressed. It also means that we've had some new, maybe even life-changing experiences. This concept can be applied to learning physical skills like riding a bicycle, playing tennis, dancing, or developing a healthy relationship with our devices. Anything we attempt to understand better, any topic we want to master, any type of exploration starts at the same entry point: a feeling of discomfort. Allow yourself to be uncomfortable, for that is where exploration starts.

Why do I spend so much time talking about purpose in a book focused on creating a healthy relationship with our devices? Because your relationship with your smartphone starts with having an aligned relationship between you and your biological nature. When living out of alignment with yourself, you are more likely to waste time in the unconscious consumption cycles that your devices offer. You will hide yourself behind black mirrors. Before you know it, you will have spent years hiding. The alternative is to open yourself to exploration and growth through discomfort, which sit at the core of our shared life purpose.

Critique, Limitations, and the Role of Morality

Since 2017, I have had many arguments with others about my definition of our shared purpose. One critique I received was that my model doesn't incorporate the idea that a life worth living has to be productive and add value to society. I believe that my model includes a healthy relationship between productivity and purpose. When we live out our shared purpose by exploring what matters most to us, we will create value for humanity.

On the other hand, I have met many people who are "productive" but who avoid exploring or getting uncomfortable, and they often seem somewhat miserable. Productivity can be part of personal development, but it can also be destructive to it. Think about meditation, which we will dive into in part III. Becoming comfortable with that stillness while being totally unproductive can be as much part of exploration as increasing productivity levels! In other words, you don't have to be productive to explore and grow. I believe that most of us end up becoming productive members of society once we become comfortable with ourselves and start exploring our lives in our own ways.

Another critique of my theory is that there are some experiences we might not want to explore or become comfortable with. What about people becoming okay with killing somebody else? I think the answer to that is that growing to become comfortable with death is part of growth, but when it comes to killing, morality comes into play.

Morality is our own, very personal system of values and principles of conduct. Thankfully, most of us think it is immoral to kill another person. But let's take a soldier who is being trained to become comfortable with death. Hopefully none of us ever have to be in a situation where soldiers are needed, but the reality is that life sometimes includes violence and death. Soldiers should be trained to do their jobs well and deal with the stress that comes with death. I use this extreme example to illustrate the point that we all live with different circumstances and moral boundaries, while also recognizing that questions of morality and war are extremely complex—far more complex than could possibly be addressed in a few short paragraphs.

That said, there is no need to give up your values and morality for the sake of your development. Just know that people have different edges. There are areas of development you won't experience, and other areas that your friends won't. It is important to recognize that some discomfort might not be a sign of a potential growth area; it could simply mean that you are hitting your moral boundaries. As long as you know why discomfort comes up, you will know if it's guiding you to a growth opportunity or simply represents a moral boundary.

I have discovered for myself that I have one hard moral boundary beyond what we would think is normal (such as not killing). I will never choose to—at least not consciously—experience anything that will deeply upset or hurt my friends and family if I were to tell them about it. I don't want to damage my relationships or hurt people close to me. I am closely aligned with my family's values, so this limitation feels natural to me, but some of you might have to transcend what your relatives would accept to fully live your purpose. You are free to choose your own boundaries, so don't feel limited by my example.

So there you have it. I believe that life's purpose is to explore, to become more comfortable with prior discomforts and lean into our fears. The result is growth and a chance to become fuller versions of ourselves.

In reality, exploring can mean a lot of different experiences ranging from helping people, to saying something nice to a stranger, to simply walking down a street you haven't explored. Exploration can take whatever form you like, as long as you are consciously choosing it. Establishing a healthier relationship with technology can unlock the ability to explore even more broadly and deeply. And when that exploration is bound by your values and sense of morality, it becomes the most meaningful gift you can give yourself and the world.

Upgrade #3: How would you live if you accepted that exploration was life's purpose? How would you interact with your mobile devices if that were the case? Growing into your fullest self will come from exploring life and your own growth edges and becoming more comfortable with what was previously uncomfortable.

UPGRADE #4: RECONNECTING TO FUTURE YOU

You are not a single personality.
You don't live just for your current self.

You are a system of integrated subsystems that make up a whole. Like a country, say the USA, many of these subsystems or communities come together to make decisions for the country as a whole.

Many spiritual communities have also developed ways of subdividing the human being into systems. Commonly, we differentiate the body, mind and soul. But the split can be significantly more nuanced. In the world of energy, the body is classified into seven chakras or energy centers. You've probably heard people talk about "unblocking" their chakras, which simply means allowing energy to flow freely so that harmony is created between the physical body, mind, and spirit.

Another way of looking at it is through Maslow's hierarchy. Maslow tries to explain the human being through a "pyramid of needs" that can be in harmony or dysfunction. Psychological, safety, belonging, esteem, and self-actualization needs are different layers of our personality that can be in completion or in harmony with each other. And then there is Freud's model of the human mind. There are conscious, subconscious, and unconscious layers working together to create the reality we live in.

And then, of course, there is the Western medical perspective, which organizes us into subsystems like the brain, heart, liver, and other organs. It is a very mind-centric way of splitting our being up.

Why does this matter, and what does it have to do with our smartphone-related habits? Tech companies are uniquely capable of analyzing and dissecting their customers to understand how to speak to us in order to capture our attention.

While each of these models describes parts of who we are, none of them is complete. After all, we are incredibly complex; every attempt to reduce that complexity will miss parts of the truth.

In a similar way, the model I am about to present to you will be a reduction of reality. This model is based on one element that is commonly underrepresented in models like the ones above—one that I think plays a huge role in the information overload and attention economy of today's world.

That element is time.

What if the personalities within us are defined not only by our body parts, chakras, or hierarchical needs but also by the temporal dimension? And I don't mean this in a cheesy way like, "All you have is this moment." I truly believe that we live in much more than just this very second. We are simultaneously reliving our past, experiencing the present moment, and imagining our future. From a temporal perspective, there are three personalities operating within us at all times: a Past Me, a Present Me, and a Future Me.

These three personas are available within us at every moment and each one has different needs and desires, especially when it comes to technology usage. As long as we are aware, we can call on experiences from the past, the present, and our aspirations for the future simultaneously. When these three are aligned and work together, like the three musketeers, we feel alive in the moment; we feel a fundamental level of well-being. But when one of them is either shut out of the conversation or dominates, we get out of alignment.

Earlier, I mentioned Dr. Jeffrey Martin, who studied people who experience "fundamental well-being". I spoke to him on several occasions and read his book, *The Finders*, in which he describes what people who experience significantly higher levels of well-being have in common. Among their shared aspects is an intriguing perception of time.

Together with a sense of inner peace, no other characteristic seems to be associated more with the fundamental feeling of well-being than a "present-moment awareness," as Jeffrey calls it. The people he studied reported a significant increase in their ability to focus on the present moment and a dramatic reduction in thoughts about the past and future. They have a heightened present-moment attention that leads to a richer experience of the present and an ability to process more sensory information.

So-called Finders can shift away from the narrating self and place less importance on their life stories and associated memories. They focus away from their Past Me and become deeply aware of or emerged in the present moment.

The key word here is "awareness," because without it, our attention will get pulled into the future or the past. First, we start worrying about the different complexities in this world. Will I have enough money for the future, will my job still exist, where will my children go to school one day? Soon you get reminded of how you had financial struggles, lost a job, and had a hard time finding friends at school. Next thing you know, your phone pings with a news notification telling you how screwed everything in the US is right now and your attention is suddenly far from your present moment, scattered across time and space. And more often than not, we are unaware that this is happening until it's too late.

With the media delivering such a negative worldview, it's natural to seek escape through your smartphone. Tech companies then have an easy path to grabbing your attention for an even longer ride. Extractive algorithms, overwhelming choice, and enticing conveniences work together to take your awareness out of the moment. All you are left with are impulsive decisions and endless scrolling into the wormholes of social media and YouTube.

Every moment spent unaware is a moment lost. Considering that the average American only has about twenty-two thousand days to live as an adult, every day truly is precious!

The problem isn't that we have multiple personalities with different needs, it is that technology has created an imbalance between them. Technology, and especially internet access through our smartphones, has made it easier for us to overemphasize the needs of Present Me. The subconscious cravings for instant gratification are enabled through the abundance of choice and the everything-right-now economy that technology is providing to us at an ever-increasing rate.

Mobile devices have put us in a hamster wheel, constantly craving more rotations and faster speeds. And while the wheel is spinning faster and faster, we forget that it isn't actually going anywhere. We start to experience life not in the moment but in the space between moments. It feels like we are in a flow state but it's like a cheap imitation of a flow state. We come out after a few minutes or a few hours not even remembering what we just watched or consumed on our smartphones. This experience is the opposite of what Jeffrey Martin describes as present-moment awareness. You could call it moment-to-moment unawareness.

As the cycle of cravings spins faster, it gets harder to stop without getting seriously injured. At some point, it is just easier to roll with it than to stop the machine and discover what we've lost. This is the tragedy of overdosing on momentary cravings made so easily accessible through our smartphones

"What causes procrastination is not the desire to avoid work. It's the desire to avoid feelings. More specifically, negative emotions."

- **Adam Grant**, a UK psychologist

I would argue that this desire to avoid feelings causes us to give in to tech cravings. But feelings are one of the most important ways that we use to communicate with ourselves! Unfortunately, tech has legitimized and is constantly supporting us looking away. For example, the feelings of numbness, dissatisfaction and regret after binge watching Netflix are real. What about the feelings of envy, depression and anxiety induced by Instagram's tendency to make us feel like we are not living up to the exciting lives of our friends or wannabe stars?

Tech algorithms want you to consume right now, not in the future. They are begging you to spend our attention with them, now. These algorithms don't care about how you'll feel later; they don't take responsibility for your digital well-being. So you have to.

"The dilemma of intertemporal choice is how to appropriately weigh future gains and losses. The trap many people fall into is being too present-biased in their preferences, which means that they allow short-term motives to swamp long-term interests. Bringing the present self into dialog with the more future-oriented self and finding a way to balance their competing concerns can help come to decisions more compatible with one's overall interests."

- **Prof. Don Moore**, UC Berkeley

You have to take responsibility for Future You, as much as you are interested in Present You in every given moment. As we already uncovered, many disappointments in life come from the difference between reality and expectation that only you can manage. If you spend your attention with social media and other exploitive algorithms, you might run out of time needed to live up to your own expectations, to become the future version of yourself that you want to be!

Refocusing on Future Me

We need to find ways to rebalance the focus between Present Me and Future Me. An aware Present Me will always incorporate the needs of Future Me. But without that present-moment awareness we are lost in this moment, constantly doing without feeling like we are progressing. The distinction between the needs of your current self and future self is crucial in understanding who you are!

Take a moment to think about your needs right now. Take a breath and tell yourself out loud what you would like to do at this very moment. Maybe you would like to watch Netflix on your smartphone, smoke some weed to relax your mind, or you are just hungry and want to eat. We all have different needs in the moment. I won't be offended if your current needs don't include reading this book. I get that. You are more likely to read this book not to fulfill one of your current needs but because you want the future version of yourself to be different.

Future Me has different expectations for itself than Present Me. This is a constant dilemma in us. The unaware Present Me wants to lay in bed and play computer games, but Future Me wants to stand up and get fit. Right now we want to eat ice cream, but our future self wants that healthy fruit bowl. Current Me desires sex, and Future Me wants a healthy, loving relationship. One seeks fun and happiness while the other strives for fulfillment.

If I had to describe the dilemma between the current self and future self in one sentence, it might sound like this: Present Me wants to be stimulated while Future Me wants to be proud of its life. The problem has never been that they both exist inside us. They are part of the human condition. But what is striking is that tech has enabled Present Me to get the upper hand so easily and so often. Present Me has been given weapons that Future Me has a hard time matching.

The incentive structures behind digital products have led to an unbalanced relationship between those two Mes, creating a winner and a loser within us.

In most moments of life, this imbalance doesn't matter to us. What is one more moment spent on YouTube? The problem is that many moments strung together are your future. They matter. In fact, every single moment matters. Not only to us but also to tech companies. We are slowly waking up to the fact that tech companies prefer to engage with our Present Me because it's the version of ourselves they have easiest access to. And so it is natural that app design will use exploitive algorithms to support our momentary cravings over our long-term desires.

This overfocus on Current Me can feel depressing. As I was writing this book, I reached out to my friend Nate, who was working on his own book, a guide to creating a happier marriage. I was curious to hear about the progress he was making.

What Nate told me instead was saddening to hear.He mentioned that his smartphone is almost single-handedly holding him back from achieving his goals. He wakes up early and is excited for the day. He makes plans, knows what he needs to do, and is genuinely interested in making progress. Then he showers and makes breakfast. He feels energized and ready to start working on creating Future Nate. But just thirty minutes later, he's been sucked into a YouTube wormhole, randomly clicking through videos. After watching close to a dozen videos, Nate told me, he feels disappointed and no longer excited about the day.

This is the power technology has over us even in moments when we're excited to grow into better future versions of ourselves. By overfeeding the cravings of Present Me, we impair our ability to balance the needs of our present and future selves.

Our smart devices have made life so convenient, so abundant with options and manipulated by extractive algorithms, that we have an increasingly difficult time balancing the needs of Present Me and Future Me. A great example of how the convenience economy has changed the balance is Netflix's transition from a DVD rental service to an on-demand video streaming platform.

You might not know or remember this, but Netflix started in the late nineties as a mail-in DVD rental service. You simply ordered the title you wanted and received it in the mail a few days later. When you were done, you returned the DVD in a prepaid envelope. At that point, Netflix sent you the next title on your wishlist.

Netflix "power users" were once the ones who watched two DVDs per week. The physical time spent for the DVDs to travel made that the upper limit. Plus, this system required the user to maintain an online wishlist of titles. Once the list was empty, Netflix would stop sending DVDs. So the user had to think of their future selves. What would a Future Me want to watch the most?

Then in 2007, Netflix launched its on-demand video platform, and its customers' usage behavior changed completely.[93] Today's Netflix users no longer have to be concerned about the future version of themselves, because the on-demand video platform feeds their current-self cravings. As Netflix grew, users became increasingly lured by the platform's convenience, clever design elements, and exploitive algorithms, which laid the groundwork for the phenomenon of binge watching.

Although CEO Reed Hastings originally conceived the streaming service as the future of online movie rentals, TV shows eventually began to take up a larger share of Netflix's streaming library, leading the company to start producing its own ever-more-addictive shows in 2013. Would you watch a trashy TV show if you had to actively order it for a future version of yourself and wait a couple days for it to be delivered? Most likely not. Netflix shows us how our preferences change when availability is instant and only the present matters.

As a side note, it is important to not mix up the needs of our future selves with the cultural context we are in. My family, for example, spends a lot of time thinking and preparing for the future, and some of them go to extreme measures to prepare for it. They wrap their TV remotes in plastic, keep things in their original boxes, and keep their belongings out of the sun. This is not what I refer to as present-moment awareness of the future self.

When I visit these family members, I find a house full of old things I would have replaced years ago because they're no longer functioning. What they are doing is obsessing over preserving them and putting weight into every single moment by being concerned about an item's future state. They are obsessing over preserving the present condition into the future. I hope that it is obvious that this type of behavior neither represents awareness of the present moment nor consideration for a future self. In most situations, it actually does the opposite, locking your future possibilities by overextending present conditions.

When you are aware of yourself, your bodily sensations and thoughts in the moment, you bring consciousness to life. By including the needs of a Future Me in the present moment, you will make strides towards fulfillment by increasing your chances of becoming the person you want to be.

Before you finish this chapter, I want you to do something for yourself. I know that most of us have a vague idea of who we want to be in the future, some understanding of who Future Me might be. In part III, we will learn about tools that combine the needs of Present You and Future You to create an untethered relationship with yourself and tech devices. Knowing who Future You will be is essential in applying the tools and techniques you will be learning.

So before we move further, set aside some time to write a letter to yourself. The letter should be at least one page long, and should be addressed to yourself one year from now. Put yourself in the shoes of Future You: Whom do you hope to be, and what do you hope to have achieved by then? Try to bring some clarity to what Future You desires.

Writing this letter is not only a way to manifest your long-term hopes and dreams; it's also a way to understand the kind of life Future You would be proud of having. Date the letter one year from now, and write it as if your life has gone exactly as you wanted it to go. Do this before reading any further.

* * *

Congratulations for openly communicating with Future You! Once you are done with the exercise, go to futureme.org and send the letter to yourself. Copy and paste what you wrote and send it to yourself. You should receive the letter one year from now. Congratulations for taking the first step towards becoming an untethered version of yourself and embracing your Future Me.

If you enjoy the concept of Future Me, I recommend reading an article on Medium called "We Need To Talk: Marriage Counseling with Capitalism Itself."[94]

My friend Renee sent me this article after she read parts of my book. It also describes the term Future Me and goes a step further in discussing what it would mean if we also thought of Future Us in similar ways, which represents the long-term needs of humanity and incorporates our kids and the earth.

The layers of your personality are timeless when they are combined and working together. Unfortunately, with the attention economy comes a focus away from Future Me into the unwanted behaviors of Present Me. Binge watching, binge eating, and undesired consumption come as the by-product. And while present-self awareness, which we will examine in more detail later, is the most sustainable instrument for dealing with temptations, sometimes it's just better to not surround yourself with them. Maybe it is time to give up your Netflix subscription, delete that gaming app from your phone, or even reduce the number of unhealthy groceries in your home to remove the temptation in the first place?

Upgrade #4: Include the needs of Future Me in the present moment to make decisions and take actions that you will be proud of rather than distracted by.

COMMITMENTS TO YOURSELF

As soon as we place our sense of self and fulfillment entirely in the external world, we are doomed to let the media and tech companies control our behavior, attention, and well-being. Our beloved smartphones are the most powerful tools we've ever owned, right at our fingertips.

But with this power comes responsibility. Unlike a hammer or a knife, this tool is not just made for you, the user; it's also something that companies and other people have access to. It gives you direct access to their services, but it also provides them direct access to your time and attention. This is why it's even more important for us to rely on our inner strength and guidance to avoid getting stuck in our smartphone's feedback loop, being guided by extractive algorithms interested in keeping us stuck against our will.

True growth and fulfillment have to come from within, and the five pre-requisites are the first five steps on that journey. Let's recap them:

Upgrade #1

Understand and accept that your brain self-inflicts negativity, that we can be attached to it and that you have the power to change some of it by understanding and managing your expectations.

Upgrade #2

As long as you haven't started taking full responsibility for your actions, you are not in control of your well-being. Commit to your true power by enabling it through curiosity and courage.

Upgrade #3

How would you live if you accepted that exploration was life's purpose? How would you interact with your mobile devices if that were the case? Growing into your fullest self will come from exploring life and your own growth edges and becoming more comfortable with what was previously uncomfortable.

Upgrade #4

Include the needs of Future Me in the present moment to make decisions and take actions that you will be proud of rather than distracted by.

You've made it this far. You accepted that you are the cause of your misery, stopped blaming others, and took full responsibility while kindling your curiosity. You have committed to cherishing your own power, understood that you have to become more comfortable with what caused discomfort before, and included the Future Me in everyday thinking to increase the chances of living a fulfilled life to be proud of.

Now we are ready to build on these first five prerequisites with tools that will take you to the next level, from smartphone dependency to full ownership of your untethered life. Understand that what follows are not just concrete tools; these are higher-level techniques and practices that we are going to tackle. Some of them, you might have already implemented in your life, while others will feel strange and maybe uncomfortable. Remember to stay curious and open minded. If you commit to those practices, you will move from smartphone overuse to being closer to having an untethered life.

Tools for Your
Untethered Life

Taiwan, an island nation just south of China with a population of about twenty-four million people, is known to be one of the cleanest countries in the world. Taiwan is also one of the few countries that had the COVID-19 outbreak under control in 2020 and became a refuge for international travelers during the pandemic. I spent several months there myself in 2020 and 2021.

But in the nineties, Taiwan had a very different reputation. It was given the unexpected nickname of "garbage island". Trash was piling up in the streets and near public garbage bins, and people were even using those to throw out some of their household garbage. Rats started to populate the city streets and Taiwan's population started to fear the outbreak of diseases caused by the unsanitary environment. Public health didn't seem to be a high priority back then.

These days, Taiwan is a model for public health and cleanliness, with one of the best-rated health care systems and highest recycling rates in the world. In 1993, however, Taiwan had a trash collection rate of just 70 percent.[95] Yes, almost a third of the country's trash was not being collected! People were demonstrating in the streets because conditions were so bad.

So how did Taiwan go from "garbage island" to a recycling frontrunner? And what the heck does this have to do with our tech usage? Let me explain, because Taiwan did something that I will ask you to do as well.

One of the first steps Taiwan took to clean its streets was to build and improve existing recycling facilities to handle the island's trash output—a logical step most governments would have probably taken. But the Taiwanese went beyond that. Instead of just solving their problems with technology, they understood that technology is more effective when paired with behavior change.

The government decided to remove most public trash bins (except in a few locations like subways) and change the way trash is collected by disallowing people to put their trash bins out into the streets for pick-up. Instead, people had to bring their trash to the garbage truck. Every evening, garbage trucks drive by while playing a song I associate with ice cream trucks in the US. It notifies people to come out and directly dispose of their trash onto the truck without leaving a trace behind.

It is kind of a cute process, not only because of the ice cream truck sound but also because it is when people of all generations leave their apartments to remove their trash together. I did it a couple of times, and to be honest it felt kind of epic. It is still an inconvenient chore, but I felt a level of social responsibility and pride while doing it.

What the Taiwanese government seemed to understand back in the nineties is an element of human nature that many of us are not fully aware of even today—that we often indulge in conveniences that do not actually serve us well! We talked about this tendency extensively in part I of the book.

Once they removed public trash bins and made people dispose of their trash directly onto the garbage truck, they made it less convenient to take care of garbage. The government involved their population in the trash disposal process and gave back responsibility to the individual, which led to a significant reduction of trash produced by each person and kept city streets extremely clean.

By removing conveniences, they increased people's awareness and sense of responsibility and improved life on the island. This whole experience made their citizens more cautious and aware of germs, which I am sure (along with their proximity to China) contributed to the country's effective response to the COVID-19 outbreak.

We too have to understand that not everything that is convenient is helpful. Just because something is easily accessible through our smartphones doesn't mean that it is actually good for us. Remember, I lost $100,000 conveniently by trading stocks from my bed…

Before the smartphone era, I would have had to call a broker, who would have likely advised me against some of my decisions and prevented me from losing so much money. The consequences of convenience can be truly damaging.

The tools and techniques I recommend in the next few chapters will not always be comfortable or convenient to implement. I will ask you to reduce some of your conveniences. I know that may be hard to do sometimes, but don't worry—I will try to make it as easy as possible. Remember, willpower alone won't help us deal with the constant distractions from our devices. Sometimes you will not have access to the great amounts of willpower needed to do what is right for Future You.

Willpower is a finite resource, and you can't rely solely on it to break your unhealthy tech habits. The tools I will be introducing over the next chapters will help you remove some of the unhealthy conveniences that tech offers, add healthier rituals, and become better prepared to deal with distractions. They will help you feel more in control and less urge to control.

The eight Rs are eight sets of tools focused on addressing all the different ways our smartphones distract us. These tools can be used regularly to create and nourish an untethered relationship with your smartphone and other digital devices while simultaneously helping you connect with yourself and those around you.

The Rs are eight action-oriented tools to help you move from smartphone overuse or codependency to a life that balances the needs of Current You and Future You while still allowing for regular smartphone use. Each R will bring you closer to a healthy relationship with your smartphone. I believe that when we resolve the complex relationship with our devices, we often uncover a new relationship with ourselves.

A quick note before we talk about the eight Rs. I will use the words habit, ritual, routine, and practice frequently in the coming chapters. They may sound like synonyms, but some writers make a distinction between them, defining habits as automatic behaviors that can sometimes be detrimental, whereas routines, rituals, or practices are things we consciously choose to do. Not engaging in a habit is uncomfortable. In my writing, I also attempt to stick to this distinction.

The first four Rs—Rank, Remove, Rearrange, and Replace—describe one-and-done setups that will help you to **prepare your smartphone** to be less distracting to your daily life and goals. These principles can—with a little adjustment—be applied to your tablet, computer, and other app-based devices as well. The Fulfillment-Based Categorization introduced in the first R could even apply to other tasks in your life. The first four Rs focus mostly on setting up your devices to improve how you spend your precious time with them. The best part is that you can accomplish all of the steps described in the first four Rs in less than an hour!

The four remaining Rs—Repeat, Remind, Reconnect, Recharge, and Reframe—describe ongoing rituals, rules, and habit changes that can be applied daily to redirect your attention to what truly matters. Instead of setup guidelines for your phone, you can think of them as **guidelines for yourself, your space, and your way of organizing time**. While the first four Rs focus on upgrading your phone to be a better partner, the second four bring attention back to you. They are intended to direct the sum of what you do every day, which defines the story of your life, to align with the needs of Future You. It is essential to apply these tools every day to stay away from smartphone dependency. You will also discover ways to set expectations for yourself, manage your happiness, and become the desired future version of yourself with the help of your technology.

I truly believe that change comes from the individual. Change comes because we want to change. Rather than relying on big tech or the government to change their attitudes toward our well-being, we have the power to define our own happiness.

And the most amazing part is that regaining control over your smartphone use does not mean getting rid of the most powerful device in your life! Don't be hard on yourself and think that replacing your smartphone with a dumb phone is a sustainable solution. You might feel like a hero for giving up your smartphone for a brief period of time, but "escapees" typically find themselves back with a smartphone within weeks, if not days. Instead of getting rid of your devices and making major life-changing decisions, let's try to understand what levers actually work and how we can set up our devices for success.

"Hope declines with experience and is replaced by acceptance."

- **James Clear**, author of Atomic Habits

I encourage you not to waste this opportunity to get your digital habits/ routines right by putting the eight Rs into action. It will take work, but with time you'll start to see the fruits of that work—a healthier relationship with tech and yourself, digital habits that feel nourishing, and a new understanding of how to make progress toward Future You.

R1: RANK

The real estate on your smartphone will define how you interact with it. If most of the apps on your phone are games, guess what? You will use the device mostly for gaming.

Some apps on my phone I use often. Others I use rarely. Most of the apps on my phone, however, I literally never use. But they keep slowing me and my smartphone down. I know that one of the reasons I had multiple screens filled with unused apps on my phone was because of FOMO. I thought I would miss something important if I didn't have those apps available at all times.

Categorizing the apps on your smartphone helps you identify the purpose they serve in your life. This ranking step will let you uncover what you are using all of your apps for and make it easy to (R)emove, (R)eplace or (R)earrange them later in the book.

The four most common ways to categorize tasks are energy based, time based, priority based and work/life based. Energy based categorization assumes that certain tasks require more or less mental/physical energy, allowing you to sort them based on how you feel that day. The time based prioritization method allows you to sort your tasks into (typically four) different categories of urgency. And the work/life based categorization, unsurprisingly, categorizes your tasks as either personal or professional.

You might ask, why invent a new way of doing things when there are so many methods out there already? The reason is that none of the common ways describes tasks in the context of tech dependency. This is why I am proposing a fulfillment-based categorization. The goal here is to identify tasks that will help you become the person you truly want to be and focus on tasks/apps that bring you joy.

And I don't just mean joy at the moment the task is being executed. Tasks can bring us joy before, during, and after. So, we shouldn't just look at an action and judge it by how fun, stressful, or energizing it is in the moment of action, but rather over its entire cycle, from the first time we think about it to after we have completed it. What provides us with the most joy before, during, and after completion is what truly matters.

A Fulfillment-Based Categorization: How to Rank Everything

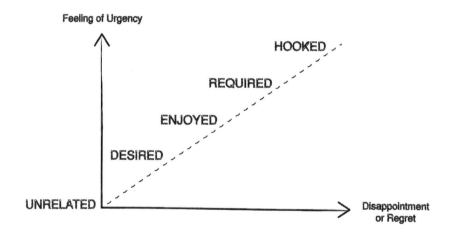

In the fulfillment-based categorization, we categorize tasks—or apps, in the case of our smartphone—by how urgent they feel before we engage in them and by how much disappointment or regret we feel about having engaged in them after the specific task. We are essentially trying to categorize if a task or app makes us happier or less happy if we engage in it. For example, when I played computer games a lot, I constantly felt an urgent need to be playing. But when I gave into that need, I wouldn't feel happy—just tons of regret for playing for so long.

The four main categories are Desired, Enjoyed, Required and Hooked. As we move from Desired to Hooked, the feelings of urgency and regret increase before engaging with the task. Also, the further up and to the right we go on this line, the further away we go from fulfilling the needs of Future Me.

In the first category, Desired, you can generally place all desirable tasks and apps, the ones that bring you closer to becoming Future You. That could be the practice of daily meditation with a meditation app, or reading books daily through Audible, or learning a new language with Duolingo. Desirable doesn't necessarily always mean fun; desirable tasks provide varying degrees of fun. For example, most people wish they were eating vegetables every day, but it's not always that enjoyable to do so.

That is why the second category, Enjoyed, exists—to group generally enjoyable tasks/actions/apps. Enjoyed is the sweet spot where we want to spend most of our time: doing things we truly enjoy. For me that is making music, making food and shaking my butt to bass-heavy hip hop, or zooming into Google maps to learn more about the world.

In the third category, Required, we place tasks that are necessary for life to function normally. Any actions you need to do fall into this category, like commuting to work, work itself (if you don't enjoy it), or your daily hygiene routine.

As you can probably already see, all of this categorization is highly personal. I enjoy cooking, but for some people eating food is a necessary task they don't enjoy, while others might have an unhealthy relationship to food. Whatever a task represents to you most of the time is where you should place it.

This leads me to the fourth category, Hooked, which is where we place our unhealthy habits and tasks. These are items or apps that are part of our lives but that we are not sure if we want to actually have in it. For me, that was Instagram for the longest time. I felt a need to open the Instagram app, only to find myself scrolling purposelessly for an hour, followed by a sense of unhappiness.

Finally, we jump back to where the x-axis and y-axis meet, where we find the Unrelated category. This is where we place tasks and apps that do not serve a purpose in our lives. Thankfully, it typically doesn't require more than a few minutes to get rid of them and speed up our smartphones and our lives.

Now that you are aware of the rankings, take a moment to take a concrete step toward untethering yourself: put all the apps on your smartphone into the five categories above. I know that some might fall into multiple categories, but be honest and choose the one that makes the most sense. When in doubt, place an app in the less desirable category to be safe.

Here is a table to fill in with names of all of your smartphone apps by category if you desire to spend a little less time on your phone. The first time I did this, I had over 140 apps on my phone, so the printed worksheet was too small and inconvenient. You can also do this exercise on your smartphone. Take out your phone and create new folders (named Unrelated, Desired, Enjoyed, Required, and Hooked) and place every app in one of those folders.

Fulfillment-Based Categorization of Smartphone Apps - Worksheet				
Unrelated	Desired	Enjoyed	Required	Hooked

I understand that the first time doing this will be tedious and maybe even overwhelming. I spent a couple of hours the first time, but after that, I usually spend only a couple of minutes bringing things up to date every few weeks. Also, you will likely end up with a lot of apps in the Required and Unrelated categories. There will also be apps in the Required category that you use multiple times a day and others you only use sometimes. That is okay, too. For now just accept the imbalance of the ranks. We will do more sorting later.

As you have surely already figured out, you can extend this fulfillment-based categorization exercise beyond just your phone and to your daily tasks, hobbies, and responsibilities. This ranking system can be applied to anything that is relevant for Future You. If you want to apply this exercise to your life more broadly, that's great, but for now let's focus just on the apps on your smartphone.

Now that you've ranked your apps, we can move on to the most important step: removing some of them.

R2: REMOVE

Many years ago, on a flight to Europe, I learned how distracted and attached to my phone I had become. I remember the exact moment when I realized that my smartphone had become much more than just a tool, something I depended on to an uncomfortable degree.

Midway to our destination, I needed to use the restroom, so I walked over, opened the door ... and immediately pulled out my phone. As for many of us, taking out my phone had just become part of the bathroom experience. But what was even worse was that this had happened on a plane. I knew intellectually that there was no internet access on the plane, and nothing for me to really do on my phone. But it still ended up in my hands, unlocked.

I remember scrolling from one home screen page to another... without doing anything at all. I opened a couple of apps, just to close them within seconds as they were useless without an internet connection. I guess the simple action of swiping and seeing all the app logos was powerful enough for me to feel like it was worth doing?

Thankfully, somebody knocked on my door a couple minutes in to help me out of my trance.

As I squeezed myself back into the tight airplane seat, I looked around me and wondered if I was the only one who experienced these trance-like states when using my iPhone. Was I the only one who couldn't resist the temptation of touching and playing with my device?

I looked to my right, where a tall man was sitting. He had just unlocked his phone and started swiping around. He had to know that most of his apps would be useless without internet access. But the swiping itself seemed to provide him with some pleasure because he swiped from screen to screen several times before finally landing on a specific app: the United app, the only one that provided free access to any internet-based content. He spent the next five minutes or so on the app, opening links and swiping around. I doubt there was much for him there, and he didn't end up watching any of the content on the app.

I started wondering: Had I done this, too? Had I used the United app just to get my fix of clicking and swiping? I opened my phone, checked my screen time, and found the proof: *United app: 9 minutes*. I didn't remember spending that much time on the app, but there it was.

As the man locked his phone, I turned my attention to the left. There was an older lady, probably around seventy, on her tablet. She was doing the exact same thing I had just seen the man do: swiping left and right on her home screen, trying to find an app she could still use without the internet. She tapped on the Google Docs app, swiped around for a bit, then opened a document I assume she had made available offline to read. She read for maybe a couple of minutes and then locked the iPad.

It wasn't just me. My tech behavior was commonplace. I wasn't the only one being lured into aimless clicking and swiping even when I knew there was no internet and no real purpose for using the device outside of getting my fix.

Most of us have experienced this kind of mindless, purposeless scrolling—the feeling of urgency and powerlessness that makes us hold onto our smartphones and play with them when there is nothing to do.

My experience in the clouds made me realize that my device had taken control of me like cigarettes do with so many smokers. I needed to touch it, to light it up and use it. It made me realize that I needed to find ways to reduce the urgency I was feeling to unlock my phone and open the apps on it. I wanted to feel less of that uncontrollable desire to play with it.

So right there, on my flight, I started taking back control. The first thing I did was to remove so-called Zombie apps, ones I had installed years before and that I never used. They fill space unnecessarily while making our smartphones (and us) look more important. They are visual clutter that not only distract us from finding useful apps, but also provide visual stimulation that keeps us on our phones even when we don't have to or want to be.

The good news is, removing these apps is pretty easy. It's so simple that I think you should do it right now! Take ten minutes now and remove the Zombie apps on your phone. You've already ranked them, so this step should be extra easy. Just remove every app in the folder Unrelated. Don't think about it too much—you can always download the app if you miscategorized it. Just do it. Untether yourself from these useless apps. Stop reading until you've removed them.

* * *

Okay, the first step should have been decently easy. You were prepared for it, and you only removed apps you weren't using. The next step will be a little more challenging.

After the airplane incident, I also decided to delete some apps I actually enjoyed using but that tend to make me feel uncontrollable urges, including some games, news apps, and financial apps that I used regularly. This was hard for me. What helped was knowing that downloading them was easy, so I decided to do it anyway just to try it out.

Thankfully, you are well equipped already because you have a list of such apps in the Hooked category. I recommend removing all of them. You can always download them later on, but for now, go broader than you think you might need to. Most of these apps don't fill a need that includes Future You, so they are great candidates for removal, don't you think?

I used to have an unhealthy habit of checking the news several times a day, scrolling mindlessly through Facebook or checking out what my friends were experiencing on Instagram. I realized that many of those behaviors were driven by the same underlying need to let my mind wander, connect to my friends and the world, and feel like I am up to date with where we are as a society. Some of it had to do with FOMO, and some of it was the feeling of being shocked by our politicians or other unexpected news that I enjoyed at a deeper level but never wanted to admit to.

Removing the Hooked apps made me realize that I was able to meet some of these needs in a different way. For example, to connect with my friends, I started calling them more often during my daily thirty-minute outdoor walks. I also introduced more play through board games and sports. I was able to reduce some of those desires through practices of mindfulness, awareness and upgrading my mindset as described in part II of this book. Uninstalling Instagram, news apps, and games from my smartphone made me feel a little naked—but I knew that deleting these apps would help me live a fuller life.

So, right now, your task is to cut out as many apps from the Hooked category as possible! If in doubt, cut it out. Uninstall the app. Remove that distraction.

I understand that you might not want to delete all the apps in this category. For example, if you placed messaging apps in here you might resist removing all of them because it would make it difficult to connect with friends. If that is the case, I recommend moving the app to the Required category.

Also, if it comes easily, think beyond your smartphone: are there other activities that fall into that category in your real life? Be truthful about the things that make you feel urgency paired with a feeling of disappointment afterward, and remove them now. Take them out of your life, and say no if they try to come back.

The first time I did this I ended up removing ninety-eight apps—about two-thirds of the apps on my smartphone!

Removing these apps or tasks might mean adding inconveniences to your life. But that is not always a bad thing, as you already know! Sometimes when things are harder to get, we value them more. By making it harder to access unhealthy behaviors, we open room for healthy ones to enter. For example, after deleting the news app on my iPhone I noticed a change in how I consume news. When I look for news these days, I catch myself reading with more curiosity on topics that matter to me rather than the topics an AI thinks I will most likely click on. The little inconveniences help me become better informed about what actually matters, rather than what keeps me engaged.

If you haven't yet, take some time right now to remove as many apps in the Hooked category as possible, preferably all of them. Do it right now.

Adding Apps to Remove Distractions

Now that you have deleted so many unhelpful apps, take a moment to recognize your good work. You just took a huge step toward untethering yourself, so take a few deep breaths and thank yourself for the work you just did.

Removing distractions goes beyond simply deleting apps on our smartphones, however. Sometimes we can remove distractions by *adding* functionality to our phone. Here are a few apps that I started using that have helped me regain focus. (I am not associated with any of those products, and don't get any benefits from recommending them):

The Brave Browser

The Brave browser[96] blocks online surveillance, loads content faster, and uses 35 percent less battery. And the most exciting part is that it maintains support for all your Chrome extensions. Your data is more private, meaning ads won't target you as much and will be blocked more often. I started using it in 2020, and it has made me enjoy my online time more by removing ads and streamlining the browsing experience.

Forest App

This app[97] is one of the most interesting ways to help you beat your digital addiction and overcome distractions. By gamifying the experience of staying away from your phone, it helps you stay in the moment. How does Forest do that? Basically, as long as you leave your phone alone, a tree will grow on your screen. Leaving the app in the middle of a work session will cause your tree to die. And the Forest team is serious about planting trees. They partner with an organization that planted almost one million trees by the end of 2020. This is one way to help yourself while helping the world.

Freedom App

The Freedom App[98] takes a completely different approach to focus compared to the Forest app. Instead of incentivizing the right behavior, the app simply blocks what distracts you while you want to focus on a task. It is available on all your devices and syncs between them, meaning you can be distraction free for as long as you want across devices.

Before I start working, I typically close out everything and reopen the apps/websites I know that I will need for my work. Then, I allow Freedom to block all other apps on my Mac, plus websites like Facebook, YouTube, and Apple News that I know will distract me. Then I can focus for the period of time I set in the app without distraction. And if I do end up on an undesirable website, the Freedom app reminds me in a mindful way: "You are free. Enjoy this moment." Thank you, Freedom app!

There are a few other apps worth mentioning. Flipd[99] is a research-backed app that hides social media apps and games from you. OFFTIME[100] lets you monitor your smartphone usage in real time. Channel[101] (iOS only) helps you to turn off distracting settings and features for the apps you use all in one place. If you catch yourself getting distracted while using the Chrome or Firefox browsers, there are three extensions that can reduce distractions: the Intention,[102] Hide Feed,[103] and Hide Likes,[104] Chrome/Firefox extensions, all created by Dan Kang, a former Googler and current digital wellness expert. Try them out and test what works best for you!

* * *

In this chapter, you deleted apps that are distraction hazards and considered adding new apps like the Brave Browser, Forest app, and Freedom app to keep your attention where it needs to be, with a focus on Future You. The third and final step of this chapter is to bring back some insights from Upgrade #1 and Upgrade #2. Remember, some of the dissatisfaction you feel comes from within, and you need to take responsibility for it.

While deleted apps can be easily reinstalled, and distraction-freeing apps provide temporary relief, to be truly happy over the long run, you have to look deeper—deeper into your own software architecture, the internal coding that is creating some of those distractions. You need to reprogram yourself, not just your smartphone. I call a tool I use to do this reprogramming and remove the cause of some of my self-created distractions the Happiness Tax.

The Happiness Tax: A Short Tangent on Removing Inner Distractions

While the first four Rs are focused mainly on how to prepare your smartphone for an untethered experience, I wanted to share a concept that has helped me eliminate some of my self-inflicted inner distractions—some of the misery I've been causing myself.

In 2017, I went to an event at which Matt Mullenweg, the founder of Wordpress, was talking about tech, his place in it, and his backpack. Yes, his backpack—something he, unlike most people, thinks about in depth. If you want to know why and how, check out his blog post called "What's in My Bag, 2020".[105]

Anyhow, Matt not only thinks about the world unconventionally, he also organizes his mind around ideas that help him show up in more productive and helpful ways. While Matt was on the podium in 2017, he gave us a glimpse into one of the concepts that make his way of thinking so exceptional. I don't recall if he named it this, but I call the concept the happiness tax.

We all know that on an individual basis, happiness and taxes typically don't go together. On average, we pay every fourth dollar we earn as income taxes to the government. Giving money to the government does not feel great for many of us, but that money does a lot of good for all of us. It enables all of the services that help us meet our basic needs. Health programs, social security, defense and homeland security, retirees and veterans, research, infrastructure, and educational spending make up the highest tax-financed government expenditures.

Basically, every fourth dollar we earn is used to create a safe and functional environment for all of us. The money is used to alleviate some of the major burdens and pains that other less-developed countries still suffer from: health problems, retirement, security, etc. In Western countries, we pay taxes to make our lives safer and easier. We pay taxes to live fuller lives. And we pay taxes so that we can make more money. Better streets, consistent access to electricity, stable internet, and fresh running water are just some of the examples of how tax money is used to enable each individual to earn more money.

But what if I told you that paying every fourth dollar in income taxes is cheap compared to the price we are currently paying on our positive thoughts? As you already know, studies claim that about 80 percent of our thinking is negative or repetitive. That means of all our thoughts, a minority is actually desirable. To have just one desirable thought, we go through four undesirable ones.

Now let me act as your mental health tax advisor for a moment. I think that paying an 80 percent tax on your thoughts is way too much, and that you would be happier if you had fewer undesirable thoughts.

The good thing is that the happiness tax provides a way to reduce that enormous mental tax bill. How? It decreases undesirable thoughts and your overall mental tax bill by introducing a smaller tax that you pay less frequently. So how do you do that?

**Consciously shift worries into support for yourself and others.
Move away from scanning for dangers to scanning for connections.**

If you want to feel more present, have a less chattery mind, be less distracted, meet more people, and develop deeper connections, give your mind more desirable thoughts by shifting to supportive thinking. The safeguards we put up prevent us from connecting with ourselves and others.

The answer lies in reducing unhealthy thoughts by worrying less and helping more. Every time you catch yourself scanning your environment for dangers, thank your mind for the thought and redirect your mind to scanning the environment for opportunities to help. Instead of creating worries and negative thoughts about how somebody or something could take advantage of us, we refocus our attention on the positive aspects of connecting with others. We assume the goodness in others and their best intent.

For example, the next time you meet a new person, be aware of your reactions to them. Do not judge their looks, their wording, or their pronunciation; do not scan for dangers. If you catch yourself doing that, shift to meet them as if they pose no danger to you. Ask them about what they do, offer them help on their way, and be a good friend before you have even developed a friendship.

At the same time, be equally sensitive to their signals; don't try to "force" anyone into a sense of safety around you. Your openness will not always be received in the way you like, and that's okay. But you may find that by shifting from worrying about danger and creating an atmosphere where people feel welcome, you will make a new friend, experience laughter and joy, and gain help when you need it from a trusted soul.

When we scan for dangers, we try to protect ourselves from harm but we also prevent ourselves from experiencing a lot of beauty. If we bring down our walls of worry, we reduce the negative effect of undesirable thoughts on ourselves and those around us. We increase the chance that something positive will happen.

Obviously, this is not always going to work out. By paying attention to your worries and shifting them into support, some of those new and old friends will see this as an opportunity to take advantage of you ... and when that happens, you will have just paid a little happiness tax. Instead of being unhappy all the time by scanning the environment for dangers, you pay taxes for your happiness when they are due. And that payment is much smaller than the 80 percent most of us are currently paying on our thoughts.

Like the processor in your computer or smartphone, your brain is constantly running background tasks that occupy a percentage of your processing power. Most negative thoughts happen unconsciously and sometimes these background thoughts can be extremely harmful. Depression, for example, can literally freeze your operating system by taking up 100 percent of your processing power. The happiness tax can free us from a portion of our undesirable thoughts, if we just remind ourselves that we are better off paying a small tax from time to time versus a big tax all the time.

The alternative is that our negative thought patterns will overwhelm our system and hinder us from being present. We can't focus or get anything done without being distracted by these other, often unwanted processes. Technology devices can contribute to those patterns by adding more worries to our lives. We worry about missed messages, or how our words came across online. We stress about whether we looked good in the last pictures we posted, and whether people will like what we had to say about our lives.

In a perfect world, we would have an app like an activity monitor for our mind, one that shows us all the processes running and taking up processing power. In that case, we could simply identify all the thought patterns running in the back of our mind and close them out, freeing up more processing power to observe and enjoy the present moment. But because we don't have that ability (at least not as of 2021!), my most effective tool has been the happiness tax.

Act as if everybody was your friend, try to help them, and shift away from scanning for dangers to scanning for connection. Expect that here and there somebody might not treat you well in return. Sometimes your kindness will be taken advantage of. Sometimes when you do something good, in return, you will be disappointed. Just accept that life gives you lots of great presents when you are scanning for connections and only asks you for a small happiness tax in return. That seems like an amazing deal!

The alternative to accepting the happiness tax is what most people currently experience: We are scared to do things because we might fail, scared to meet people because we might not like them or think they could hurt us. Our risk aversion is costing us happiness and contributing to that 80 percent of repetitive negative thinking.

If we as a society have agreed that taxes are necessary, can you convince yourself that it is necessary to pay a tax on your happiness in order to create a higher capacity for it? Accept a small happiness tax to avoid paying a much larger mental health tax, and you will get much more back than you can imagine.

R3: REARRANGE

This is weird to admit, but like most cats, I have an obsession with boxes. I love them because they help reduce clutter, keep things organized, and most importantly, make it easy to move items around.

But there is also another, more personal reason I love boxes: my mum.

My mum is incredible. I love her so much (even more than boxes). But my mum doesn't love boxes—she loves bags. She uses paper and textile bags to transport her things, and it has always bothered me deeply. Do you know that one box, like one piece of luggage, can fit a dozen of those bags? My mum has what I call a *tiny little thing syndrome*. She likes to carry her life in little bags.

To put it lightly, I hate the thought of transporting many little bags around when one big box will do. Most summers growing up we would drive from Austria to Croatia, where my mum's family lives. I loved spending time in Croatia at the seaside but I hated getting ready for it, because it meant that I had to deal with my mum's bags, stuffed by the dozens into the trunk of our car. Sometimes she had so many that we had to put the overflow into a cargo box on top of the car. Some bags had just one single item in it.

It drove me nuts. And it still does. I can feel anger coming up when I think about her tiny bags. I guess that's why I don't like grocery shopping—it reminds me too much of chaotically carrying bags to Croatia.

But, like most unpleasant experiences, this one brought something truly useful into my life. I discovered how useful boxes can be to keep my life organized and tidy. And not just in the physical world, where I store many of my life's possessions in large boxes, but in the digital world, too. So how can the idea of boxes help us rearrange our smartphone apps so that we feel more focused and less overwhelmed?

Boxes: How to Rearrange Your Apps

In the Rank chapter, we learned about five categories of tasks: Unrelated, Desired, Enjoyed, Required, and Hooked. These categories are basically boxes for our apps. They were useful in the Remove chapter when we got rid of the Unrelated and Hooked apps. After removing those apps, we can now focus on arranging the remaining three folders.

We unlock our smartphones dozens of times every day. What we see after that unlock, the home screen—another box—looks very different for most of us. Whatever it looks like, though, it is incredibly important that the apps you show there are the least distracting and most useful. Thankfully, since iOS 14—and most current Android versions—an app does not have to be visible on your home screen pages to stay installed on your phone.

Apple seems to understand the value of boxes, and has used them to create a way to easily find all your installed apps. With iOS 14, when you swipe all the way to the right you'll find a new screen that Apple calls the app library. Your apps are automatically sorted into categories there and will stay there as long as the app is installed on your iPhone. Look at all of those beautiful boxes!

Apple's got you covered—but there's still more you can do to rearrange your apps to be as undistracting as possible.

My preferred way of opening an app and avoiding getting distracted by the rest of the beautiful apps on my phone is the swipe-down search function (swipe-up on Android). On your iPhone's home screen, swipe down from the top to reveal a window that allows you to search for an app by typing its name. It's a great way to have a less distracting experience while on your phone.

This means that on iOS 14+ you can remove an app from your home screen and still access it by swiping down on any home screen page to search for it, or swipe all the way to the right to reach the app library containing all installed apps. On Android, there is similar functionality when swiping up. When you try to remove an app, you are given a choice to either remove the app from the home screen only or to delete it from your device.

You can now take a minimalist approach by limiting yourself to just one home screen page. How? By only showing the apps that you truly want to see, the ones you want to use more often.

Obviously, those will be the apps in your Desired category. So the first step is to place all the Desired apps you truly want to be using and that bring you closer to your future self on one home screen page. For many people that includes meditation apps, podcast apps, and other self-care apps. This is where I have the Forest app and the Freedom app, as well as my fitness apps.

Place these apps in whatever order you want on your home screen. Don't use folders if you can avoid them; you want these apps to be immediately visible after the unlock, but you can put them in folders if they don't fit onto one screen. Your home screen should now show all apps from the Desired category and two folders (Required and Enjoyed).

The second step involves apps in the Required category. This may need a bit more work because it is likely your biggest category and contains a much wider range of utility. Some of the apps in this category you might use once a month, while others, like Google Maps or your browser, you use multiple times a day.

I recommend placing your most used and most useful apps in this category into the dock—the bottom row of apps that doesn't change when you swipe to another screen. In case you utilized the Fulfillment-Based Categorization Worksheet, use a highlighter or pen to mark those apps before moving them. The dock on my iPhone is only able to take four apps, so I decided to put them into folders and move them there.

When I did this step, I identified fifteen Required apps and moved them from the Required folder into my dock.

The final step might surprise you. I removed all the remaining Required apps and Enjoyed apps from my home screen. Meaning every app in the two folders Required and Enjoyed—and the folders themselves—I removed from my home screen but not from my device. These apps are still available through the search bar or in the app library, just not visible on my homescreen.

If you followed these three steps you should be left with only one home screen page showing your Desired apps and the dock showing your favorite Required Apps. Isn't that pleasant to look at?

It is worth mentioning that some of my essential Required apps, such as Twitter or Facebook Messenger, might land in somebody else's Hooked category. For me, neither causes habitual use or uncontrollable distraction, but it could very well for others.

If you are using iOS 13 or lower, follow the first two steps. Then, instead of deleting the Required and Enjoyed folders, simply move them to a second home screen page. Do not take the apps out of the folder—just leave them in there to reduce visual clutter. Feel free to arrange the apps within the folders if you feel the need to; I favor looking for them in the search bar.

If you haven't yet, take a moment now to rearrange your apps.

You might ask yourself: What do I do when I download new apps? Won't this mess up my organization? If you were successful in removing and rearranging apps, then you should be left with a single home screen. In that case, every newly downloaded app should land on the second home screen automatically. Leave them there for a few days, maybe until the end of each month. Then, at the end of the month, rank, remove, and rearrange those new downloads, effectively removing the second home screen again. This should take a couple minutes max.

Congratulations! Your apps are now all boxed up, and you are three quarters of the way through organizing your phone! These were some huge steps in creating a less distracting smartphone experience for yourself. I am sure this fulfillment-based categorization will help you to align more closely with the needs of Future You.

* * *

With awareness and curiosity, we can better understand each of the boxes that surround and contain us, whether it is the country you were born into, the parents who raised you, or the technologies that define your experience every day.

While I don't know your parents and how they influenced you, or how the place you live has shaped your life experience, we all share some common aspects of being human. We are all influenced by a fast-changing, complex world and biased by sensationalist media outlets.

We are under the spell of digital technology, spending more time with it than directly with other humans. It overwhelms us with choice and convenience and makes us less attentive. But as we start to understand the box of technology at a deeper level, we can unlock a more fulfilling, less tethered life—one that doesn't come with the constant need to check your phone.

R4: REPLACE

In some cases, your desire to watch videos or scroll endlessly on social media will be reduced by simply removing or rearranging apps. But that is not always the case. Some of that desire will likely persist even after you execute on the first three Rs.

If you removed the Facebook app, you might find yourself logging in to Facebook through your browser more often. Even the inconvenience of doing it through the browser might not influence your usage behavior a lot. For some of us, deleting the app will do the trick all together, while for others it might just reduce our usage by a few percentage points.

When an app serves the needs of Present You but not those of Future You, it can be dangerous to get sucked into it. But what if you could replace that app with one that meets both of those personalities' needs? That's what this chapter will help you do.

I had to do just that with my YouTube app. First, I deleted the app. But a few days later, I found myself regularly opening YouTube in my browser. And although no longer receiving notifications from YouTube did reduce my consumption, it was still hijacking my attention for an hour per day. Although using the browser was annoying, it didn't reduce my YouTube consumption by as much as I'd hoped for. It did go down by about a third, which made me feel happy but still not like I was satisfying the needs of Future Me.

Then I discovered the golden rule of habit change.

This rule says that the most effective way to shift a habit is to find a competing response to an old trigger.[106] If your current boredom routine involves opening Youtube, TikTok or open social media apps—and you want to change that—you could either try to always stay busy or change your reaction to being bored. Staying busy at all times might be impossible and also unhealthy. So what would it look like to find a competitive response?

I started to wonder what need was underlying my YouTube usage. I realized that often rather than being hooked on watching videos, I was enjoying the content, the pieces of knowledge presented to me in most of the videos. Some of my YouTube consumption was pure entertainment, but some was also learning, which is why I had such a hard time giving it up.

So I decided to download Audible and place the Audible app exactly where I used to have my YouTube app on my homescreen. I opened the app and downloaded a bunch of fiction and nonfiction books, and then it happened… I started organically replacing my YouTube use with a Future Me-approved app. Suddenly, instead of wasting my time, I felt like I was learning and making Future

Me proud by consuming content that I knew would help me.

Although removing the YouTube app only cut down my usage by a third, replacing the app with Audible cut my YouTube use further—by way over 50 percent after just a week and by about two thirds just two weeks in! Plus, instead of constantly having to resist the urge to open YouTube, I found those urges reduced because Audible was meeting a wider range of my needs.

Most of the time, our bad habits are a way of dealing with stress, boredom, and unmet needs, so eliminating them can be very hard. It is doable and should be attempted, but relapse can happen. However, when successful, breaking a habit will open yourself up to a new way of being. And when eliminating it simply isn't working, or when we want to supplement the elimination through a better ritual, we can replace the app that is causing the bad habit with one that supports a healthier one!

All habits, good or bad, are in our lives for a reason. We invited them in, consciously or not. For example, opening Facebook first thing in the morning might make us feel connected to our social network. But it is also likely to divide our attention, overwhelm us, and reduce our productivity. At least we feel like we are caught up with friends, right? Each habit provides us with something, or we wouldn't be doing it.

The great thing about replacing is that it even works at the level of tech devices. For example, you could replace some of your smartphone usage with a Kindle. At home, I like to place my Kindle on the table so that it's convenient to open it instead of my smartphone when I feel the need to engage with technology. Whatever is within your reach and vision is more likely to be used. We will talk more about placement in the sixth R, but in general, I recommend keeping whatever you want to be using within your visual field.

So, you have ranked all your apps into five categories, removed the ones that don't serve you, and rearranged the rest. Now let's take some time to replace some of those apps with ones that serve your needs better.

Identify the apps that most serve the needs of Current You and that you feel an urge to use. They could be apps from the Hooked category that you've hopefully deleted. If you still find yourself using those apps frequently through the browser, they might be good candidates for replacement. Take a few minutes to identify apps that can be replaced and brainstorm which apps you could replace them with. If YouTube and Netflix provide you with entertainment, what else could fill that need? If Facebook and Instagram are your problem children, what else could make you feel connected?

Identify up to three apps that you are still using habitually and that do not serve you. If you decide to replace them, try to position the new app where the old app used to be, but still keep everything on a single home screen page. Placing the new app where your fingers used to go to open the old app allows you to use the bad habit for good. I understand that this could lead to a slight deviation from our fulfillment-based categorization, but it can help significantly with problem apps, like YouTube was for me.

Studies suggest that relying on willpower alone to keep a new routine will only work for some people.[107] Removing an app doesn't make it disappear from your mind. But strategies like replacing that don't require us to be strong all the time can help change toxic habits into healthy ones. With about 43 percent of our actions being habitual, it is important to identify them and cultivate behaviors that serve us better. In the next chapter, we will dive deeper on this.

In summary, when we make bad habits more inconvenient, the friction it creates can help us move in a new direction and even create a new, better habit. I believe the power of habits is one of the most underrated forces in our life.

In the fifth R, we will move from talking about how to set up your devices and dive into how to not only avoid bad habits but also create routines for your untethered life.

R5: REPEAT

Congratulations! You are halfway through the 8Rs—and you have just reached the most exciting of the Rs for me. While the first four Rs are focused on adjusting your smartphone, this chapter is all about doing the right things for Future You over and over again.

Starting with the fifth R, we will explore the Right daily practices to create an untethered life. Daily practices are so crucial because every action we take either moves us one step toward or away from who we truly want to be. Every action we take is either Right or Wrong. Right brings you closer to who you want to become, and Wrong takes you further away. Right actions are effective in moving you closer to Future You.

Right and Wrong are capitalized to make it clear that I'm not referring to something done in the right/wrong or efficient/inefficient manner, but something that's inherently helping or hindering you in achieving your goals.

For example, let's say you enter a hot dog eating contest. You win the contest by eating more hot dogs than the other contestants in a certain amount of time. Congratulations! You did what you were supposed to do in the contest; you competed in the right way. But what if your actual life goal were to become a fast sprinter? Entering a hot dog eating contest might not have been the Right step toward that goal.

Similarly, your goal may be to get better grades in school or university. Maybe your goal is to start a company from home. But when you sit down to do your homework or make progress on your startup, you keep checking the notifications on your phone every few minutes. Ultimately, you lose hours of work time due to mindless scrolling. This is a huge disservice to Future You.

With every action you take, you consciously or unconsciously decide whether to stay on course and become the desired version of yourself, or travel in the other direction, away from Future You. Every action that takes you closer to your future goals—as long as it's moral and in integrity with yourself—is a Right action, whether it's executed well or not.

One of the biggest fallacies we fall into is what I call the "efficiency fallacy." Doing something well feels good temporarily. I enjoy being efficient, so I desire to complete more tasks efficiently, and perhaps even choose tasks based on how efficiently I think I can complete them. That means that either the Right or the Wrong path can feel good temporarily, as long as we feel efficient and productive along the way.

If I had to rank what feels most satisfying, then obviously I'd rank doing the *Right thing right over doing the Wrong thing right*. But unfortunately, I would also rank doing *anything* right over doing the Right actions wrong. And this is the problem. Doing things badly does not feel good most of the time, but it is a necessary part of becoming who we want to be!

For example, say you sit down to do some challenging but important work that you're just not excited about. To escape the chore, you open Instagram. You post a story that then gets one hundred views and ten comments. You just did the Wrong thing right by successfully publishing content, but it didn't get you any closer to your goal of completing that difficult piece of work.

Clearly, taking the Right actions toward our desired future matters, but our ego also cares about doing things well, whether they're Right or not. In addition, for most of our educational and work lives, somebody else tries to define what is Right for us, whether it's parents, friends, lovers, teachers, coworkers, and even random strangers on the internet. Many people expect us to behave in certain ways, and most of these ways are not Right for us.

So the truth is, the few Right ways for us are not competing with a singular Wrong way—they are competing with a large number of Wrong ways.

Making time to take the Right actions toward Future You should be your daily focus. Otherwise, it is more likely that your ego or other people's expectations might misguide you. This chapter will describe two techniques that will help you make progress on your path even when you're bored or unmotivated and inclined to fill mental space with mindless scrolling and time wasting—selling your mental space cheaply in a vicious cycle of social media engagement, TV binge-watching, video gaming, and constant smartphone checks.

Left to our own devices (literally), we indulge in many Wrong activities. More often, we take the action that is most available/convenient to us, and we execute it efficiently. So how can we make sure that we stay on track when motivation is low or we feel boredom? How can we escape this technology trap?

I want to share the two concepts that help me the most in staying on track toward the goals of Future Me.

Accountability Buddies: Staying on Track with Friends

Did you know that according to research from the University of Scranton, just 8 percent of people achieve their New Year's goals?[108] There are many reasons for this, ranging from setting resolutions that are too ambitious to reprioritizing goals, but I believe that overreliance on willpower and a lack of accountability are the main reasons we fail.

As personal technologies have become more powerful over the years, I've realized that I cannot rely solely on my willpower to act in accordance with Future Me. A growing body of research is starting to prove that resisting repeated temptations takes a mental toll.[109] Willpower gets depleted over time. Thankfully, I've found a solution, a win–win situation where I can simultaneously help myself and my friends stay accountable toward their future while they help my Future Me.

Since COVID started, I have had a daily practice of working with accountability buddies. For one hour in the morning and one hour in the afternoon we meet over Zoom to work together toward our future goals. We spend the first five minutes stating our goals, work on them for another fifty, and then close out the session with five minutes of review and feedback.

Setting aside two hours a day for this practice is not realistic for most people. But even if you work a regular nine-to-five job and have other responsibilities, implementing an accountability buddy practice before or after work, or at least on the weekends, will accelerate you into the Right future.

In addition to having work sessions with an accountability buddy, I also created a short and simple check-in practice with another friend that only takes less than a minute to complete: It's a four-line text we send each other each night that (1) lists the date, (2) summarizes how successful we were in establishing/maintaining routines, (3) states whether we achieved the goals we set for the day, and (4) shares new goals for the following day:

3/16/2021
  Habits: :)
  Achievement: :(
  Goal: Reduce my screen time by one hour

If I'm satisfied with my overall practices (mental, physical, spiritual)—let's say above 70 percent of what I want them to be—I'll give myself a smiley face in the "Habits" line. If I achieved the goal I set the day before, I'll give myself a smiley face in the "Achievement" category, or if not, a sad face. And finally, I'll write my goal for the following day.

I recommend starting this practice by creating a list of daily routines you'd like to practice. This list will help you gauge your success in the "Habits" category and guide you to more smiley-face than sad-face days. You can supplement these texts with weekly or biweekly calls with your accountability buddy to discuss your habits and goals. This short texting practice keeps me accountable and aware of Future Me on a daily basis.

If you cannot think of a friend to partner up with, you can find accountability partners at Focusmate.com[110] or Flow.club.[111] These sites are used by a wide range of people, from high school students to famous authors—I ended up having a session with Nir Eyal there twice—to get work done together with other humans. Imagine them like workout classes for your brain instead of your body. Also check out my website, TheUntetheredBook.com, where you'll find challenges to transform your life with the use of technology, plus ways to connect with other untethered creators and work together as accountability buddies.

The first step is to become aware of and set goals. I do this together with an accountability partner at least once a week, typically on Sundays. Once you know your goals, social accountability increases the chances of achieving them significantly—even more so when you commit to one person in particular. If someone devotes their time to you and helps you succeed, we feel like we owe them something in return. That something is our commitment to our own goals.

As you replace your old anxiety-inducing habits with practices that serve Future You, smartphone distractions will feel increasingly irrelevant or uninteresting. Working with accountability buddies is a wonderful and accessible version of such a practice. You'll connect more closely with a friend and improve your focus. A regular accountability routine will help you become more of the person you want to be and be less concerned with missing out on distractions. I can think of no better use of your time.

Scheduling Time Alone: Staying on Track by Yourself

I no longer wait for a feeling or inspiration to become Future Me—I block off time for it in my calendar. The things that we do not prioritize, that we think we will do once we have time, are the ones that get hardly any time allocated to them. If we don't make time for important relationships or tasks, those relationships won't flourish and tasks will never get completed.

Scheduling can be used as a practice to align with the needs of Future You. This step alone, I believe, could enable you to grow into the person you are proud of, the person you want to be.

We tend to schedule time in our calendars for important relationships so those relationships don't wither. We all know the dangers of a lack of social connection: socially disconnected people are less happy and healthy, and they live shorter lives.

Many of us do not schedule alone time. But if scheduling our friends helps us develop closer relationships with them, why wouldn't scheduling time alone also support us in developing a deeper relationship with ourselves and our Future Mes?

By scheduling time with yourself, you are making it a priority to live up to your values and future needs. We have all the tools we need to organize our lives and prioritize our values, but why is it still sometimes so hard to organize ourselves around our priorities?

One reason might be the always-on culture and channels that our smartphones provide to us. FB messages, WhatsApp, SMS, Instagram, TikTok, and email are all direct ways for other people to access your time and attention. When you react to the incoming stream of notifications, you are essentially giving up on your priorities to satisfy the needs of Present You. Scheduling time with yourself is a practice that moves you away from distraction and toward your priorities, closer to the desires of Future You.

I have adapted the ritual of scheduled time in most aspects of my life. Scheduling is so important to me that I've even developed some guiding mottos around what activities should be scheduled. They are:

1. Schedule everything that would have required driving before the internet existed. Watching movies, buying groceries, and whatever else we used to need to leave the house for should be scheduled in the digital world, too.

2. If it takes less than five minutes, do it now! Don't schedule tasks that take less than five minutes to do. Just do them!

3. If there are many little tasks, work on them in one session. Tasks that take more than five but less than fifteen minutes can easily be done together in an hour of focused work. Schedule those hours in your calendar and add an agenda to the calendar entry.

4. Be flexible. But schedule that, too! Add time to your calendar for random things to come up.

5. Use schedules as guidelines, not hard rules. Scheduling should liberate you, not make you your calendar's slave. If you are in flow during one task, reschedule others. Don't fight the natural flow of productivity.

Logically, every slot in your day that is not scheduled is free to be occupied by whatever or whoever screams the loudest, which can be useful or counter-productive. (Smartphones scream very loudly!) That is why during my scheduled time I don't react to any of the always-on channels on my tech devices. I don't look at messages, I don't respond to emails (unless I am scheduled to do so), and I don't respond to incoming calls.

I know these rules are easier said than done. It can be challenging to not respond to messages from friends or work emails when social norms dictate that you should be available at all times. It's not that you won't respond to messages and emails; it's simply that you now have a designated time set aside each day for these tasks. We will talk about how to best manage your availability to others later in "Limit When Your Attention Is Up for Grabs."

There is one exception to my rules about scheduling time, and it is when I schedule time to give in to the needs of Present Me. I might end up chatting with friends, talking to my parents, doing laundry, lying in bed, being playful, or just going for a walk. I simply listen to myself and then allow Present Me to decide what play it wants to engage in. It is healthy to play as long as it is a choice that you are making out of a position of pure desire to play rather than escapism from one reality of life. Play to have fun, not to run away from something.

The tool I've found most valuable for scheduling is one you're most likely already using: Google Calendar.

Every Sunday, I sit down and review my plan for the next two weeks, to make sure that I'm focused on the Right things. I spend about fifteen minutes looking at the time I've scheduled with others, as well as the time I've scheduled for myself. Also, every day after I wake up and go through my morning routine, I spend a few minutes with my calendar and my journal—more on both in the upcoming chapters—to schedule my day with others and Future Me.

The most important feature for me in Google Calendar is the ability to share my calendars; it allows me to include accountability partners in my scheduling so they can hold me accountable for my goals. In Google Calendar, sharing your schedule is super quick. After opening your calendar, select the three dots next to your calendar name (they appear after you hover over the name). Then select "Settings and sharing," where you will find the option to either create a shared link to your calendar or directly add email addresses to it.

Scheduling time with myself and working with accountability buddies have become cornerstones toward my untethered life. I enjoy adding new events to my calendar and making sure I stay on track toward Future Me. By learning how to use scheduling in a way that makes the most sense for me, I was able to find joy in it rather than being stressed out by it. As long as you schedule time for what matters to Future You and leave flexibility in your calendar for whatever life brings your way (or your own state of flow), you will get fulfillment out of it.

If you want to upgrade your scheduling skills, I recommend reading Neil Fiore's *The Now Habit*. He has studied how to create and follow through successfully with new habits. He spends an entire chapter talking about scheduling and left me with some important takeaways on how to schedule effectively that I've adjusted to my needs and started incorporating into my life:

1. Color code your calendar. He uses red for fun so he can see easily how much fun he had during any given week. If you want to get deeper into color coding, I recommend starting with Calendar.com CEO John Rampton's blog post titled, "How to Color Code Your Calendar for Optimal Success."[112]

2. Schedule non-work activities first.

3. Before you do anything fun, spend a couple of minutes scheduling a work-related activity or an activity that Future You would be proud of.

4. Schedule work blocks instead of large projects; it is more motivating.

5. Never end down! Never stop when you are in a tough spot. Stop when you feel good about where you are at. Stay with the difficulty, or start on the next section before you quit so that starting is easier next time.

If you follow my mottos and the insights from Neil's book, you will more effectively focus on the needs of Future You and be more efficient in moving toward your goals.

* * *

Working with accountability partners and scheduling alone time are the two main techniques that help me make use of my time and minimize distractions. Tech overloads us with information and the need to make decisions. Techniques like these help us reduce the number of decisions we have to make and help us do the Right things more often. What better tools could you ask for on this path to becoming your best self?

Up next, I'll talk about the six daily routines that help me find more attention and focus by reducing the time I spend with my smartphone. I have always been slightly reluctant to prescribe exactly how people should reduce their smartphone time because I believe that exploration is the purpose of life and the best way of finding out what works for you. The second reason I tend to withhold my recommendations is that it can be overwhelming to implement several changes at once.

For example, we find it more encouraging when we implement one major change successfully than when we manage to introduce three out of five, because we've still failed at two of them. So I would prefer that you take on what you can instead of trying to implement every recommendation I give you. Nonetheless, I understand that we all have time constraints in our lives, more so now than ever before. We want to understand what works before we give it a try.

In the next chapter, I'll share six ways to naturally reduce the amount of time you spend with your phone, while cultivating healthy digital habits. You can use the tools from this chapter—accountability buddies and/or scheduling alone time in your calendar—to make sure you get started with the practices described in the next chapter.

R6: REDUCE

"Every goal is doomed to fail if it goes against the grain of human nature."

- James Clear

What I want to discuss in this chapter is how we can support one of our most limited resources, willpower, by reducing online stimuli. When we feel drained from a long day or are simply not feeling 100 percent, we cannot rely on our willpower to help us overcome distractions. If we rely on willpower to reduce toxic behaviors such as doomscrolling or binge watching, we are likely to run out of it quickly. How do we reduce some of our toxic digital habits without draining our willpower?

James Clear, the author of *Atomic Habits*, believes that to achieve our goals, without relying solely on willpower, we need habits and routines that support those goals. According to Clear, sticky habits have four characteristics: they are obvious, attractive, easy, and satisfying. He refers to these characteristics as the Four Laws of Behavior Change.[113] They are a simple set of rules for creating good habits (or breaking bad ones by inverting the rules).

Here is a simple example of how your smartphone applies these four laws. First, your phone vibrates (obvious). You become curious to know who wrote you or why (attractive). You carry your phone around and take it out of your pocket to check (easy). And finally, you solve the problem by reacting to the notification, which gives you a feeling of relief and achievement (satisfying).

Clear's framework helps explain why our smartphones are such success-ful habit-creating machines. We carry them everywhere we go, so all they need to do to engage with us is ring or vibrate. If we wanted to break some of our smartphone habits, how would we use the laws of behavior change to do that? We could:

1. Make the distraction invisible. We could not bring our phone with us or — more realistically — turn off notifications except when real people, not businesses, are trying to get in touch with us.

2. Make it unattractive to pick up. The easiest way to do this is to put ourselves in situations where looking at our phone is looked down upon. That could mean hanging out with more people who value offline connection without distraction.

3. Make it harder to respond. This could mean making it more difficult to read a message by not showing its content on our lock screen, putting our phone far away, deactivating face or finger ID, or requiring a long PIN code to unlock.

4. Make it unsatisfying. You could put your phone in an ugly or uncomfortable case that you don't enjoy holding, or turn colors off, for example.

In this chapter, we will apply the four principles of behavior change whenever possible. That said, if you feel one of the techniques is not sticky enough, try to first enhance it by making it (more) obvious, attractive, easy, or satisfying before giving up on it. What feels satisfying to me might not be satisfying to you, so there is room for personalization.

On another note, before I share the six Reduce techniques with you, understand that there are endless articles online on the topic of tweaking your smartphone settings to help you use your phone less. Recommendations might include setting your phone in grayscale mode to reduce visual stimuli, using silent mode to reduce the need to check your phone every time it vibrates, and disabling app notifications to reclaim your attention. I hope you understand that I won't be talking about most of these quick fixes in this chapter, because many of them don't support a healthy relationship with your smartphone. For example, of the three mentioned, I only use silent mode.

Instead, I want to share with you six techniques that will help you gain control over some of your toxic habits by reducing the time you spend with your mobile devices. These techniques will reduce your need to use willpower to fight technoference[114] and support your autonomy to make Right decisions. These techniques will help you reduce the distracted time and increase the focused time you spend with your smartphone and other digital devices.

1. Reduce Environmental Distractions: Set Up Your Physical Environment for Digital Success

Your willpower is limited, so if you are relying on it every day to control your habits and resist your urges, you are setting yourself up for failure. Instead, you can adapt the design of your environment to support healthy digital habits. In the Repeat chapter, we talked about the utility of having established rituals. It is easier to maintain those rituals when your home and work environments are aligned with your needs.

Let me ask you this question: What experience is your living room designed around? Most American households design their living room around the TV. Couches, chairs, and tables are placed in a way that they support our watching experience. Because the living room is structured to be conducive to watching TV, we end up watching TV a lot. For the average American, TV is still the primary way of consuming media.

What would a living room look like that supports you having more desirable experiences? Because you bought this book, I will assume that watching more TV is not appealing to you. Maybe you would enjoy using your living room to read more books, host friends more often, or simply stretch more frequently. What could a living room look like that supports desirable experiences by making them more visible, more convenient, and more enjoyable?

> "The most important thing we have is our attention. It's the basis for our thoughts, feelings, and actions, so it's crucial that we protect it and design our environment in ways that will serve us rather than exploit us."

- **Dan Kang**, creator of the Intention, Hide Feeds and Hide Likes Chrome extensions

Structural intention—structure created with the intention to support one's goals— is much easier to rely on than willpower. In fact, we have utilized this concept already in our very first R. In Rank, we talked about how to structure and redesign our digital environments, specifically the home screen of our phones, to engage in more desirable experiences. Having distractive applications front and center reduces our ability to be indistractable. The same principle holds true outside of digital environments. Let's talk about how we can design our physical environment to reduce unhealthy digital habits and to be more conducive to present moment awareness.

Where do you charge your phone? Next to your bed or on your desk in sight and reach? The "mere presence phenomenon" describes how the presence of one's phone alone can impact our cognitive performance and even the perceived quality of social interaction. Researchers at the University of Chicago discovered in two experiments that even "when avoiding the temptation to check their phones—the mere presence of these devices reduces available cognitive capacity.

Moreover, these cognitive costs are highest for those highest in smartphone dependence."

Having these distraction machines next to us at all times is like holding candy in front of a child's face. I understand why we would want them close to us, just like I understand why a kid would prefer the candy to be next to them. But I hope you can also recognize that it might be beneficial for you to keep the distraction farther away. It can literally increase your cognitive capacity.

The simplest way of achieving that is to have a charging station, easily accessible but also far enough away from your desk and your bed so that you have to stand up to reach your mobile devices. You could even make this behavior satisfying by coupling it with a pleasant experience, like eating a snack or listening to music. There are seemingly endless options to create a reward for Right behaviors.

If you have charging cables plugged into many outlets around the house, you will find yourself hooked to your smartphone more regularly. Also avoid having a chair or a comfortable sofa next to the charging station. It shouldn't be designed like a charging bar where you have drinks and give your phone some juice too. It should be rather uncomfortable to stand there for extended periods of time while your smartphone is plugged in. Don't hold your tethered phone if you are trying to become untethered.

If you find yourself spending too much time at your newly designed charging station, here is another trick that works, guaranteed. If you cannot separate your work space from your charging space, make it impossible for you to actually use your phone. Here is how I achieve that: I remove my ability to use my smartphone by turning it into a webcam.

Much of my day—when I do not work with an accountability partner in person—I spend on zoom calls or video calls with accountability buddies. During that time I use my smartphone as a webcam. I place my smartphone in a stand and connect it to my laptop or desktop computer through an app called Camo.[115] This neat trick allows me to integrate my phone into my environment while taking away my ability to use it unnecessarily. Minimizing the Camo app leads to the video feed disappearing, which would be immediately noticed by the other side.

We've spent a little time talking about creating an intentional working space, but there might be more to uncover here. I urge you to explore how to create a distraction-free workspace for yourself. I also wanted to address the bedroom. According to Wikipedia, a bedroom is "characterised by its usage for sleeping." Assuming that you do not use your phone to help you sleep better, why would you bring it into your bedroom? Try this: Make your bedroom a smartphone-free zone. Yes, you can have a simple alarm, of course! But challenge yourself to make your bed a device-free zone for the next week and pay attention to the quality of your sleep.

What else can you do to set up your environments for success? In addition to removing some items, you can add others by putting what Future You desires in plain sight. For me, that means having a journal on my desk, in reach and in sight. So whenever I want to record a thought or journal about my experiences, I can pull out the notebook to record it on paper instead of using my smartphone. I also place books in reach of my desk and bed so that if I do desire to get distracted, at least I can pick a medium that has value for Future Me.

Think of your physical environment as one of the primary sources of support for your digital behaviors, one that can help boost your willpower rather than drain it.

2. Reduce Stress and Number of Decisions: Establish a Morning Routine

I wake up with a different thought pattern and set of emotions every day. Sometimes I feel tired after eight hours of sleep, and sometimes I can't even sleep for eight straight hours because I have so much energy. No matter how I feel, having routines increases my sense of control over the state of my mind and body.

Before implementing a fixed morning routine, I was faced with several decisions first thing in the morning: What do I do first today? Should I sleep for a little longer? What will I make for breakfast? And so on. I was communicating uncertainty to myself right after waking up. Oftentimes, I would delay making a decision by reaching for my phone and scrolling through Facebook, ultimately leaving me in more distress once I'd emerged from the screen's numbing effect. As we already know from Trend #4: Abundance of Choice, having too many choices actually decreases freedom and increases decision-related stress.

During my first year and a half at Apple, I decided each morning which bus I would take, which depleted some of my energy. In my last year at the company, however, I took the same bus every morning. This little change helped me feel less drained and more certain every morning. I knew what the first ninety minutes of my day would look like, and I did not have to think about them at all.

This made a huge difference. Ninety minutes equates to close to 10 percent of our waking hours. Reducing my brain's processing load significantly for those first ninety minutes of my day saved energy and allowed me to make better decisions for the rest of the day. That's huge. Basically, I am giving my mind space for inspiration instead of taking space to make decisions. Also, as most of my morning tasks are routines, my mind gets time to relax and wander, to get lost and be creative rather than make decisions.

And when I say "most," I mean it. The first sixty minutes of my day are basically replicas of each other. I eat with little variation (but very nutritiously) and I take care of my physical needs. I also meditate and journal during that hour, which I will talk about in detail in the eighth R. I hardly make any decisions, and I allow my mind to ramp up slowly. No decision anxiety, no cognitive overload.

I don't want to prescribe an exact morning routine for you because I truly think that you need to establish one that works for you. I personally try to minimize my technology use in the morning, but if you want to use tech to keep yourself accountable I recommend using **Autopilot**,[116] which makes it easy to stick to your intended routine by telling you exactly what to do in step-by-step audio instructions. The app comes with tons of morning best practices, or you can customize your own.

In the eighth R, we will talk in detail about some important elements of such a routine. If you want to know more about morning routines and understand how they could be key to a successful and focused day, I also recommend you read *The Miracle Morning* by Hal Elrod.

3. Take a Break from the Always-On Culture: Establish a Boring Quiet Hour

My friend Mario Herger, a multi-book author and technology trend researcher, urges his followers to "stay bored." Boredom is the opposite of engagement. Mario describes five types of boredom. While boredom usually carries a negative connotation, and some types of boredom can induce anxiety, there are good types of boredom that can be pleasant or desirable and are essential to the success of Future You. The type of boredom in which you can let your thoughts wander and stay open to new ideas can be an extremely satisfying, relaxing, and creative space.

We can think of boredom as the state of mind in which some ideas are born. It may be an uncomfortable or unfamiliar experience at first. But, once you schedule your days to include time to let your mind wander, you will find that you're able to produce new thoughts, ideas, dreams, and connections. Think of all the humans who came before us and the extraordinary inventions and ideas they created by practicing the appreciation of a quiet and undistracted mind, free of addictive technology.

It is impossible to "stay bored," to wander and explore, when we are constantly reaching for our phones. Our smartphones are like a steady drip of morphine, numbing us just enough to not have to feel anything—least of all pure, unadulterated boredom. By removing the uncertainty that drives us to scroll mindlessly, and by creating routines that include time for our minds to wander, we can reduce anxiety and reconnect with our creative minds, producing untold benefits for Future Me.

"Ideas emerge when someone frees their mind to wander—this often doesn't happen in day-to-day life."

- **Jessica Livingston**, Founding Partner at Y Combinator

Whether it's before breakfast, during your morning routine, or in the hour before bed, doesn't really matter. What is important is that you spend some time—preferably an hour—every day disconnected from your devices. I have heard other digital habit experts recommend a day per week or a weekend per month. But I find an hour per day easier to implement and a more realistic commitment for most people. I personally find screen-free eating to be the easiest way to introduce some boredom into my life. This simple presence practice has also noticeably changed how much I enjoy the act of eating and tasting food.

One of the best ways to maintain a great relationship is to give it space from time to time. This is true for friends or romantic partners as much as it is for our relationship with our smartphones. By untethering yourself completely for one hour every day, you invite in boredom and other feelings/sensations you might have been avoiding. You set up healthy boundaries with your mobile devices. This will foster your growth, help you regain focus, and save your eyesight in the long run! Obviously, you could make this part of your morning routine.

If starting with a full hour feels unrealistic for you, try putting aside two fifteen-minute slots a day for this practice. You can start with a smaller chunk of time and expand it as you get comfortable with being untethered.

4. Limit When Your Attention Is up for Grabs: Establish Healthy Tech Boundaries

Technology has given us access to information and people, seemingly cheaply. But if you look below the surface, you'll find that the price you're paying is that everybody now seems to have access to your time as well. Being available to others probably has some benefits in your life. But being reachable twenty-four/seven comes with downside effects on sleep, recovery, attention, and your overall mental health. Being always on also means being constantly disconnected from the real world. Establishing a quiet hour every day can support in reconnecting with yourself and your surroundings.

But even when you disconnect, your friends and colleagues do not. Meaning, they will continue to ping you when you are trying to take a break. At some point, the question becomes: do you truly want to be conveniently accessible at all times of the day and by all people/companies? I assume the answer is no. So then it doesn't make sense for our phones to be on at all times, vibrating away and distracting us, right?

Our phones may stay on for twenty-four hours every day, but we cannot. As in any healthy romantic relationship, you would hope that your partner sleeps at similar times to you; otherwise, living together can become challenging, and the relationship may not be sustainable in the long term. But because your tech doesn't have to sleep, you need to force a break when you rest. Put your phone in flight mode when you are trying to be offline. And try turning it off at the end of the day, which provides another huge benefit: you won't start your day by checking your phone.

You can also try limiting the hours during which you are accessible to people. You can do that by first categorizing everyone into three groups according to the importance of being reachable by them): **essential**, **important**, and **unimportant**:

- Every person in the **essential** category has access to your attention at all times (except when you sleep), so there should be very few people in there. Mine are siblings, life partner, and parents.

- **Important** includes all people and colleagues you are open to communicating with multiple times a day.

- **Unimportant** is where you put the rest. These are people you should plan to engage with at a maximum one time per day.

How do we put this all together? Go through your contacts and define who the people in the **essential** category are. Click on their contact card, edit the contact card, and set their ringtone to "emergency bypass." This group of people will be able to reach you as long as your phone is on, even if you have a "do not disturb" setting enabled.

The **important** category includes most of your close friends. Instead of setting your phone up with special rules for those people, I recommend defining two or three time slots every day during which you allow yourself to answer them. At all other times, your smartphone should be in silent mode, if your job or obligations allow for it. The next time someone from this group contacts you, I recommend informing them about the daily time slots you set up to respond in.

It might feel uncomfortable to tell your friend that you will only be available to answer their messages and calls during certain hours, but what may not be obvious initially is that this is an act of love toward them and yourself. How?

Because you're giving them certainty. They will know when to expect to hear back from you. It's a kind act of service toward your friend and yourself, a win–win situation for both of you.

Finally, just a couple words on the **unimportant** category. The people and companies you decide to classify as such are not inherently unimportant or of lower value. You are just deciding to attribute less of your attention to them. The average American considers between one and two dozen people their friends. But there are another 328 million Americans out there. Naturally, most people you know will fall into the Unimportant group, so there is no need to individually pick and choose who falls into this category. I recommend setting up one time slot per day where you answer their messages, emails, and calls, preferably during working hours as you might have to communicate with businesses such as electric or gas companies during that time.

Define when your attention is available to others by (1) turning off your phone when you are not available at all (like when you're sleeping); (2) defining the people you want to give daytime access to you; and (3) creating a couple of time slots to respond to important people, and one time slot per day for the rest.

With iOS 15, Apple introduced a "Focus" mode to help you limit when your attention is up for grabs. Focus mode lets your friends know that you are busy, and lets you choose which apps and humans are still allowed to disturb you during that focused time. You can even use this feature to customize what your phone looks like in different situations.

5. Reduce the Effects of Technoference: Show Respect for Yourself and Others

Focusing on your phone instead of the person in front of you in a social situation is known as "phubbing." Whether or not you find it disturbing that phubbing has become so pervasive, in 2016 a few researchers published a study attempting to understand this phenomenon.[117] They found that phubbers are more likely to exhibit low self-control and high levels of FOMO, and they are higher on the scales for compulsive behavior around the internet and their smartphone.

None of these attributes are very flattering, and if you imagine a person exhibiting them, your first thought is likely not going to be, "They seem awesome.

I want them as a friend."

This fifth rule is simple and powerful when it comes to avoiding phubbing and consequently improving your relationships with your friends. When you are in the company of your friends or family, do not use your phone. Don't check your messages, don't answer calls, don't pull out your phone to look at it. Unless you all agree that your phone is needed to perform a certain action—like looking up a recipe together or watching a video together—show respect to yourself and others by keeping your phone away from your own hands.

I believe that phubbing will one day become as uncool as smoking at the dinner table. You can be a pioneer by starting to practice presence with others when in person, thereby reducing the effects of technoference on the relationships that matter to you.

There is another reason to keep your phone out of in person interactions: to enable the creation of strong ties. Most social media platforms mainly support the establishment of bridging social capital which means weak, distant relationships that allow primarily for information sharing and knowledge transfer. In person we get a chance to develop bonding social capital—strong ties—more easily than online. Bonding social capital refers to strong relationships that allow for emotional support, that build trust and companionship.

Live by the rule that your in-person friends have priority over any online connection that might be competing for your time, including your connection to your phone itself. Show your friends that you are living an untethered life and prove to yourself that you can refrain from using your phone when you're with others. Be respectful to them and yourself.

Your friends and colleagues will notice the difference when they speak to you as somebody who is fully present with them. By keeping your relationship with your smartphone separate from the relationship with your friends, you will deepen those friendships, remove distractions, and be the kind of person people want to be around. Finally, when you do need to use your phone in a social setting, acknowledge it and remove yourself from the conversation before doing so.

6. Minimize Unaware Moments: Put Pride and Joy to Work for You

The last Reduce technique is a little different than the others, which are focused on reducing time with tech as a method to minimize distractions. This technique is super simple and breaks my unhealthy habits in moments when I am already on a device — specifically in moments when I am more likely to be distracted. I call this method the Consciousness Reminder.

My "distraction danger zone" — the time when I easily get distracted — is typically between 5 pm and 10 pm each day. I know that after the sun goes down and I am done with most of my work, I am more likely to engage in unconscious smartphone usage. To avoid mindlessly scrolling or watching YouTube videos for very long, I take advantage of two of my core desires for my future self, and I use one app to help reinforce it:

- First desire: I want to be proud of myself and what I do in life.

- Second desire: I want to have a lot of fun and experience happiness and joy.

- The app: Yapp Reminders[118] (other reminder/alarm apps could work too).

Between 5 pm and 10 pm each day, I ask my smartphone to remind me of what I truly want to do while spending time with it: to have fun and do things I am proud of. I know my smartphone has its own will when it comes to what we should be doing together, but I want my voice and ideas to be heard. It's just that sometimes, I forget to listen to myself because of the great options that my smartphone presents to me. I get distracted from what matters to me. The Consciousness Reminder helps me use my mobile devices to remind me of what I truly desire.

How does my phone do that? It is super simple. Through the Yapp Reminders app. Between 5 and 10 pm, my smartphone sends me random notifications to remind me of what matters to me and potentially take me out of a distracted moment by asking me if I'm either (1) proud of or (2) truly enjoying what I am doing right now.

Every time I get one of these notifications, it acts like an invitation for my consciousness to become more present in the moment. And when I snap into awareness and realize that what I am doing is not making me proud and/or happy, it's much easier to stop what I am doing and refocus my energy on something more productive or meaningful.

Consciousness Reminders received during your weakest moments can be an excellent way to invite your awareness back. They take advantage of a behavioral psychology principle originally discovered by psychologist B.F. Skinner called random rewards. He discovered in his experiments that one of the most effective ways to motivate repeated behavior is to make rewards appear at random times. I believe that making Consciousness Reminders appear at random times can be an effective way in activating our awareness.

For me personally, pride and joy are major drivers, but you could obviously choose other drivers and questions that have more meaning to you to create your own Consciousness Reminders and increase awareness of your tech usage patterns.

* * *

Let's recap the rules one more time. First, set up your environment to make it easier to reach for what Future You wants and not your smartphone. Second, create a morning routine that helps reduce decision load on your brain and the need to use your smartphone to "figure it out." Third, set aside a quiet hour every day to be without your phone. Fourth, limit when you give your attention to others by categorizing your contacts and adjusting your schedule accordingly or simply using Focus mode on iOS. Fifth, reduce technoference, and show respect for yourself and others by being cognizant of how and when you use your phone in social situations. And finally, create Consciousness Reminders by using a notification app like Yapp Reminders to jolt you back into your present purpose.

To know whether you've successfully implemented these six tools, iOS's Screen Time can be useful in tracking changes in your phone usage over time. When it comes to measuring the quality of your smartphone usage, though, things get trickier. Screen Time statistics won't correlate your well-being with the time spent on particular apps. I am sure that in the future we will have better software and hardware to tell us when an app makes us unhappy, but for now we have to rely on ourselves to notice negative impacts on our well-being.

Beyond just present-moment awareness, noticing also requires tracking changes over time. Tracking involves establishing the right goals and keeping tabs on how we spend our time. One of my favorite tools for identifying my goals and staying on track is my bullet journal. It is a method of journaling focused on capturing and tracking changes, reflecting on experiences, and adjusting goals.[119] Tracking yourself is the best way to know whether you are succeeding in establishing new routines and following your goals, and bullet journals are highly adjustable to your individual needs.

I'll share more on awareness practices in the next chapter, and details on my journaling practices in R8. For now, know that bullet journaling is a proven method to track progress toward your goals, remind yourself of the needs of Future You, and use your tech with more awareness. Used in combination with the Screen Time feature, it can help track and reduce time spent unconsciously or in unhealthy ways.

Finally, a word of caution. Often when we try to change a negative behavior, we end up in a "yo-yo diet" situation. This can happen when we rush to extremes, take on too much, and don't find healthy and balanced ways to incorporate behavior change into our lives. It may work for the short term, but eventually we go back to eating the same junk we were eating before.

That's why I urge you to find ways to make these six techniques work for you. Experiment with them, maybe try one of them at a time, adjust them to your needs, and keep track of what works and what doesn't. But most importantly, remind yourself that you can make life easier and more untethered by fostering an internal and external environment that inspires the behaviors you want to practice. This is also a great opportunity to remind yourself of the mindset upgrades we've already gone through. You have a chance to tackle the source of some of your misery with the help of these techniques.

Even if you are not able to fully give in to your rituals initially, over time they will become routines/habits and you will feel an obligation to them. Keep repeating them. Avoid slacking by working with accountability partners and your calendar. There is so much freedom in that commitment. Freedom from decision-making anxieties and fear of missing out are just some of those benefits.

"Working on long-term projects needs the strategy of a marathon runner, not a sprinter."

- **Neil Fiore**

Avoid workaholic tendencies that can burn you out, like working uninterruptedly for eight hours on a weekend. Becoming your Future You, a person you can be proud of, is a marathon. Don't overwork, but don't procrastinate either. Stay focused, but don't burn yourself out, or you will quickly seek escape again in the alerts coming from your phone. Instead, stay curious, and keep exploring to find what works best for you!

R7: RECONNECT

The first 6Rs are my most effective toolboxes in managing information overload and unhealthy digital habits. They help me eliminate, replace or reduce undesirable behaviors and lessen the effects of information overload and decision making strain. By focusing on the Right actions more frequently we decrease the amount of stress experienced. The tools described in the first 6Rs focus on reducing stressors or digital distractors.

R7 and R8 will increasingly focus on improving our resilience to stressors or digital distractors by reconnecting more deeply with ourselves. Instead of just minimizing the number of distractions, what if we could also become more resistant to existing distractions and deal with digital disturbances without losing focus? The idea here is that by building higher resilience to distractions we stay uninterrupted even when others feel disturbed.

Imagine a horizontal line called the Distraction Overwhelm. As long as the accumulated amount of digital disturbances lies below it, we can experience high levels of focus, autonomy, and even digital health. Once the line is crossed, we become drained and stressed. By becoming more resilient to digital disturbances, we can raise the Distraction Overwhelm line and improve how we cope with digital distractions and stressors.

How do we do that? Mainly by reconnecting with ourselves, others, and to some degree the universe at large.

Unfortunately, many of us are disconnected. As we know from the last R, most social media platforms support the establishment of bridging social capital, which is weak and distant relationships. Close relationships, on the other hand, help us feel belonging and make us happy on a core level. I mentioned this before, but about 34 percent of our fellow humans walk down the street with a smartphone in their hand.[120] It makes us feel more comfortable and in control. But when a man and a woman walk together, the number goes down to 18 percent. Connection to each other apparently reduces the need to connect to our smartphone.

A 2019 poll from YouGov, a polling firm and market research company, found that 30 percent of millennials say they feel lonely and 22 percent say that they have no friends.[121] So while it is easier than ever for younger people to connect, why do millennials feel less close to each other than older generations did? A 2015 review of seventy studies showed that loneliness increases the risk of dying by about 26 percent.[122] If we know how important relationships are for our well-being, why does it sometimes seem as if tech has made it harder for us to build them?

Friendships are undoubtedly crucial for mental health and building the resilience needed to cope with distractors. Just a single ten-minute call with a friend every day can have a tremendous impact on your mental health. I personally target at least thirty minutes of reconnection with friends every day. This is an easy and effective way of boosting your mental health.

Aside from nourishing your friendships, I want to talk about four other specific ways that can help you improve your digital—and real-life—coping skills every single day by reconnecting more deeply with yourself and the world around you.

Arigato: A Practice of Gratitude and Reconnection

Ken Honda is a best-selling author with more than seven million books sold who has surveyed over twelve thousand millionaires about the unique beliefs that give them their edge.

Ken believes that the distance to happiness is relatively equal regardless of your circumstances. While research shows that a minimum level of income is needed to maximize our capacity for happiness, Ken believes that money is not the main problem—it is our relationship to it and to ourselves. While having enough money to take care of your basic needs and wants is crucial for well-being, I believe the method of Ken's I'm about to describe can apply to anyone.

Gratitude is at the core of Ken's teaching, which he calls "Arigato your money." (Arigato is the Japanese word for "thank you.") He has developed a simple mantra he calls, "Arigato in, arigato out." Thank your money when it comes to you and when it leaves. The key to a healthy relationship with money is gratitude, as it is to a healthy relationship with yourself and friends. I believe that Ken's mantra can provide a powerful balance when literally 80 percent of our thoughts are negative.

"If you appreciate what you have, it opens a door to happiness."

- Ken Honda

When money comes into your life, say thank you, and when you spend it, when it leaves your life, send it with gratitude. "All the money circulated with love, care, and friendship is Happy Money," says Ken. When we don't know how money controls us, we are stuck in the trap of needing to make more, so we become slaves to it. By appreciating what we have and supporting the natural flow of money as it comes in and goes out, we will be happier.

How to Arigato with Ease

The technique is super simple. Arigato your money—appreciate it whether it's coming or going. The next time you buy a product or any service, take a moment to speak (or think) appreciation for the financial transaction. According to Ken, this technique allows you to establish a circular flow that allows money to flow through you with blessings, grace, and ease. With that, you eliminate your stress and anxiety around money and you are to see more money come in, Ken believes. What you appreciate, appreciates you!

Similarly to Ken, I believe that many of the problems we have with technology come from deeper-rooted issues with ourselves and our relationship to others. That's why what Ken teaches about money also applies in other areas of life, like relationships. Appreciating and nourishing the ones you have, showing gratitude to your friends, and letting go when it is time to go separate ways all feel liberating and deeply connecting.

You can apply this technique in those three categories of your life: wealth, health, and relationships. When you drag your body through a hard day of work, thank it for being so productive and capable. After you play sports, appreciate your body for performing and staying free of injury. And when you think of a friend of yours, call them and appreciate them for who they have been on your journey. Instead of always wanting more from our body or mind, we can look for ways to appreciate what they are giving us every day. Wouldn't we all gain from deepening our social connections and our connection to ourselves in this tech-centric day and age?

I also want to add another category. Start thanking your digital devices, because it's kind of miraculous how much value they provide us every day. Most of the internet-connected devices we own today would have been considered magical just a century ago. Millions of human minds are coming together to create the devices and internet-enabled experiences we rely on every day.

But we take our tech devices for granted, and direct so much anger at them. We tend to demonize our devices for some of our misbehaviors and addictive tendencies. And while our devices can nudge us in certain directions, at the end of the day, we are still the decision makers.

That is why I believe that, even when we feel hijacked by the algorithms driving our favorite social media site, we should thank our devices for teaching us a valuable lesson about our tendencies. So start appreciating your smartphone for the beautiful pictures it takes, or your laptop for all the wonderful knowledge it saves, or your tablet for the fun and entertainment it provides. You will open a door to a happier relationship with your devices.

Another benefit I have experienced from thanking my smartphone after using it is that it establishes a mental sense of closure. I feel less urgency to unlock and use it again right away. And Future Me will surely arigato Present Me for using it less.

If it helps, feel free to utilize the Yapp Reminders app—or a similar app of your choosing—for this. I bet you'll remember to show gratitude more often if a notification were to ask you what you are grateful for.

I don't believe that we can create healthy relationships with other humans when we blame them for our misery, so how can we establish a healthy relationship with our devices when we continue to blame them and fail to thank them for their service? Thanking our devices for all the beauty and connection they bring into our lives is essential to healing our relationship with them and establishing healthy usage patterns. I love my devices and respect them for their powers, even if they distract me from time to time. And I thank them for the joy and utility they bring to my life, every day.

Creating Present-Moment Awareness Through Meditation

The "monkey mind" is a Buddhist term referring to the restless, confused, indecisive, or raging mind. The one that seems to always ramble, never stop, and is easily distracted. Over time, an overactive monkey mind can lead to mental and physical fatigue and divided attention. The monkey mind lowers our Digital Overwhelm line. And extensive digital tech use tends to feed the monkey mind by giving it even more to worry and think about. We can increase our resilience by slowing the monkey mind. And no tool that I know of is more capable supporting that goal than meditation.

"Work with the reality that you experience directly within the framework of your body from moment to moment."

- S.N. Goenka

In September 2016, I had my first experience with insight meditation. After just the first hour I already felt calmer, more relaxed, and more present. Once the reentry into my physical body was complete, I started noticing a difference in how I showed up to the world and how the world responded to me. The world no longer seemed to be passing by me in a continuous sprint. There was a feeling of peace in any given moment and an acceptance of the now as it is right in this second. The continuous stream of worries and hopes for the future disappeared. I had fewer expectations for myself. What mattered was being here right now. It felt like I had a small awakening experience.

I had more control over my chattery mind and was able to give the present moment most if not all of my mental capacity. In a more spiritual way, it felt like my mind, body, and soul were here together at the same time. It felt incredibly peaceful to experience this alignment. There was no place to be, nothing else to do other than what I was doing, and nobody else to be other than who I was at that very moment.

I know that if you have yet to try meditation, some of what I just said may sound a bit hokey. In Upgrade #1 we talked about expectations and how they can negatively impact our future well-being. Meditation is one tool that allows you to experience the moment for what it is and thereby lower your expectations. Let's also remember Upgrade #4, in which we explored Past Me, Present Me, and Future Me in alignment. When we have balance between the three, we feel some fundamental well-being. When one dominates, we feel distress and anxiety. Meditation can bring us closer to that experience of life.

Before I found meditation, I didn't fully understand this balance or the concept of "being present." I heard that phrase a lot, but it didn't hold much meaning. I really wasn't even aware that I had been allowing my mind to race and panic, because I didn't know that I could slow it down in the way meditation allows.

Once I was able to slow my mind, however, I realized that my anxieties about the past and future were so constant that I just thought they were the norm, like a fish in water. And every time I escaped into my screens, it was at least in part because I just wanted to not feel that anxiety anymore. Meditation is a way to recover from that constant need to escape.

Three years after my first meditation experience, I embarked on a ten-day vipassanā silent meditation retreat. Three days were given to the practice of anap-anasati, intended to increase consistency and precision of attention. The rest of the time was given to the core vipassanā practice, in which the meditator attempts to move through the body, paying attention to the various sensations that arise without reacting to them. Basically, all we did was meditate, sleep, and eat. I jokingly refer to it now as a military boot camp for awareness.

While these ten days were physically and mentally difficult, no other practice has helped me uncover my true self like vipassanā. In full honesty, this book would probably not exist if it hadn't been for my first vipassanā retreat in 2019. There, I gained the present-moment awareness, clarity, and motivation to develop a daily meditation practice to help me achieve this milestone.

But don't trust just my experience. Endless researchers have confirmed that meditation and a deeper experience of the present moment can have significant health benefits. Neil Peterson, for example, who investigated and wrote about more than one thousand psychology studies, says that "people's time perspectives correlate with life satisfaction, anxiety and depression ... people who live in the present are more satisfied with life on average, the opposite seems to be true for those who dwell on the past."

Unfortunately, we often choose to escape into our digital devices. Although happiness lies in the present moment, we try to avoid being present regularly. Our smartphones have become so convenient that we sometimes choose them over our own happiness!

How to Kickstart Your Meditation Practice

Starting your meditation practice is more straightforward than what you might think. The first step is to schedule some time every day—let's say fifteen minutes to start with—to be with yourself and only yourself. It is essential that this be a time without your phone. You should not touch or look at your phone during these fifteen minutes; put it on silent or powered off in another room or in a drawer. Sit with yourself, quietly, without doing anything else at all. Eyes can be closed or open.

Pay attention to who you are when nobody talks to you or interferes with you, when you have time to truly listen to yourself. This is an opportunity to get curious about yourself, while also practicing self-responsibility, as we discussed in part II. Meditation is a very potent tool to experience every moment for what it is, rather than what our mind is often making it to be. When you are present, you become aware of desires within you. That is the power of meditation!

The tricky part with meditation is that your monkey mind will try to fight it. You need to ignore that resistance and just do it. Meditate at the same time, same place every day. Know that your mind will likely never be excited about meditation. I know from many practitioners that even after years of meditating their chattery mind will sometimes try to talk them out of it, which makes sense considering that meditation quiets that part of our brain.

In some ways, you are entering a battlefield against your monkey brain every time you meditate. Your mind wants to consume and think more, while you are trying to calm yourself and listen to what lies deeper to have a more embodied experience. Meditation is only easy when you have no other choice but to do it.

So make sure to schedule it in your calendar every day at the same time. I recommend that to be in the morning, as part of your daily routine, because every other time in the day is more prone to be influenced by unexpected events. If you start skipping your practice, you will continuously slip out of it more. Create consequences for slipping. A friend of mine donates $10 to a cause he doesn't support every time he misses a day of meditation. Do what you need to do to make this practice your top priority.

Here are the seven steps you can use to kickstart your practice right now:

1. Schedule fifteen minutes a day in your calendar. Every day. Even weekends.

2. Before you start, set a fifteen-minute timer. This will be plenty to work with.

3. Sit down in a comfortable position. Use a backrest if needed.

4. Close your eyes and bring your awareness to your breath.

5. Experience the breath going into your nostrils and lungs. Feel the inflow and outflow of your breath. Try to focus all of your attention on it, and try to experience all the detailed sensations that come with it.

6. When your mind wanders, which will happen every few seconds, you need to do one thing. Every time your mind takes over and pulls you into the land of thinking, your only job is to pull yourself back into experiencing your breath fully.

7. Refocus on your breath, and keep your attention on the sensations that come with the inflow and outflow of it. In addition to focusing on the sensations of the nostrils, nose and lungs, you can also feel the sensations of the incoming and outgoing breath on your upper lip.

Do this for just fifteen minutes every day. If you have already scheduled your daily quiet hour as advised in the sixth R, try to meditate then. The present-moment awareness that you are fostering will give you a fighting chance against urges to throw yourself into the distractions of your smartphone. While it won't help you succeed with that all the time, the newly gained awareness will help you choose more consciously, which is a huge step toward an untethered life.

If sitting quietly with yourself for fifteen minutes feels too difficult, think of actions you already take in the morning that could be used as meditative experiences—taking a shower, walking the dog, or making your morning coffee. Designate this time to the practice of mental stillness. Instead of listing all the things you need to do that day, or repeating worries you have, remind yourself this is the time to be present. Notice how the water feels on your skin, or how the coffee cup feels in your hand.

Or, perhaps you feel like you need a structured practice with more guidance. I recommend Oprah and Deepak Chopra's 21-Day Meditation Experience.[123] They provide audio meditations, tips, and tricks to deepen your meditation practice each day, journaling exercises, and perhaps most importantly, a schedule to keep you on track. They also have an online community, where you could find an accountability buddy. The only disadvantage I see is that you have to use your smartphone for it.

Finally, you might be the kind of person who gets the most out of jumping right into intensive experiences. If you are one of these people, I couldn't recommend a ten-day vipassanā meditation retreat more highly. It will undoubtedly change your relationship with yourself and, as a consequence, with technology. To book a ten-day retreat, go onto the dhamma homepage[124] and find a course in your area. Depending on the site, you could be attending the course with either a couple dozen or a couple hundred other students, so make sure you choose what fits your needs. After the retreat, I guarantee it will be much easier for you to incorporate meditation into your life.

If you are interested in learning more about vipassanā, the short YouTube video titled "How to Practice Vipassana Meditation in five minutes" explains how you can start your own vipassanā meditation today.[125] On YouTube, you'll also find an incredible TEDx talk by Eilona Ariel showing how and why she created a documentary on vipassanā by travelling the world visiting meditation centers and prisons.[126]

Whether you choose to do a ten-day silent meditation retreat or commit to practicing quieting your mind while you drink your morning coffee, meditation will be an invaluable tool for you as you reconnect to your inner world and the present moment and encourage a healthier relationship with technology.

Clearing Your Mind with a Journaling Practice

Meditation is my primary tool in creating present-moment awareness through embodied experience. But I like to supplement it with techniques that provide similar benefits—and even enhance the meditation experience itself. One of those techniques is journaling. The act of writing down my thoughts helps me organize my mind, express emotions, relieve stress, and inspire my creativity.

While there are infinite ways to journal, like the bullet journal method I use daily to set goals and track progress, my favorite way of journaling to start the day is called Morning Pages. It's a technique created by Julia Cameron and is described in her 1992 book, The Artist's Way. This practice has changed the way I think, work, and create by helping me release the distracting thoughts that make me want to escape into my phone. Cameron created Morning Pages to help artists overcome the voices within that spew negativity.

Think of it as writing a journal but with a different purpose. When journaling, your goal is typically to capture some thoughts you have about a specific topic. It could be used to describe a wonderful day you spent with friends, help you work through a breakup, or get your newest business idea down on paper.

Morning Pages are kind of the opposite. They do not contain a specific topic, and they don't need to be remembered. Sure, if you want to remember some of the content, you can. I rarely ever look back at my morning journals—maybe because I like to delete them periodically—but have done so regularly with my regular journal.

So how does it work, and what can you get out of it? With Morning Pages, your goal is to simply write every thought you have for a certain amount of time. This ritual helps clear your mind and open a path for greater creativity. It feels different from meditation, where you are stopping and gently steering yourself away from thinking and into an embodied experience.

The practice is simple: I write for fifteen minutes without pausing about whatever comes to mind. If nothing comes to mind, I write that nothing comes to mind. But I never stop writing. Think of it as a stream-of-consciousness writing ritual. It is the first thing you do every morning after maybe brushing your teeth or having your coffee.

In my practice, I do it right before meditation. Why? Because it clears my mind and prepares it for a deeper meditation session, a greater sense of embodiment, and deeper connection to the present moment. I enjoy journaling as one of the first things every morning. Our brains accumulate tons of thoughts by dreaming. And when you wake up in the morning, your brain is clogged, whether you are aware of it or not. Morning Pages are a way to dump some of that information our brains accumulate at night for a new experience in the present moment.

The other benefit I have experienced is that it allows my mind to plan ahead. Sometimes, these writing sessions end up being more than just rituals to a clearer mind and greater awareness; they become productive sessions that help me get through the day more efficiently. You remember how I told you that I don't like using my mind actively for planning in the first ninety minutes of every day? Sometimes, my mind just wants to organize information during my Morning Pages, so I end up planning my day, organizing stories that came up while dreaming, or creating a to-do list of items I had seemingly forgotten about. The great thing is, it doesn't require me to be active in planning—my brain just wants to empty itself out!

I understand the dilemma you may be facing by being asked to add thirty minutes to your already busy mornings (fifteen minutes of Morning Pages followed by fifteen minutes of meditation). But trust me when I say that getting rid of all the distracting and anxiety-producing thoughts that overwhelm you first thing in the morning—the same thoughts that make you want to escape into your smartphone—will give you a sense of accomplishment and productivity that carries into everything you do that day. Chances are, you are already spending thirty minutes scrolling aimlessly in bed before getting up anyway, so replace that scrolling time with this practice. You will prepare yourself to make more Right decisions and be more efficient in executing them.

How to Kickstart Your Morning Pages

Here are the steps I take to write Morning Pages:

1. Choose a tool. For many people, that is an actual journal; for others it is software. I played around with different tools and ways of doing this and realized that convenience and speed are the most important for me, so I just use the Notes app on my smartphone or Mac.[127]

2. Same as with meditation, before you start, set a fifteen-minute timer. This will be plenty to work with.

3. Throw writing rules out the window. Simply write about whatever comes to mind. Do not correct yourself or worry about grammar or spelling. Align with your mind; don't try to control it and follow it where it leads you.

4. If you go blank for some time, use writing prompts. That could be thinking through your day, goals for the next year, and things you're grateful for. Just be careful not to make it focused only on those topics.

5. After fifteen minutes of writing, try not to look at it again. Don't read it or try to interpret it. Take notes on the plans or ideas you wrote about if you like, but in general, I make it a practice to delete my Morning Pages afterward.

I will always be grateful for my friend Kim Han, who introduced me to Morning Pages. This practice changed my ability to write, focus and connect to what exists in the present moment. I hope you add it to your morning ritual together with mindfulness meditation.

Even if you don't practice this precise method of journaling, I hope you'll consider finding a journaling practice or other methods of clearing your mind that work for you. Writing is a cathartic and energizing tool that helps foster the mental clarity and self-reflection you need to truly untether.

Reconnect Through Movement

For most of my life I was a very active person. I went to the gym every other day and played tennis a couple times a week. This held up until my early thirties, when my motivation to challenge my body through physical exercise started to fade. I became less active, stopped going to the gym altogether and felt the consequences of it pretty much immediately.

While my weight did not change much, my body composition did: less muscle and more fat. I started getting moodier and had less energy for everyday activities. I needed to sleep more, and the quality of my sleep worsened. I wasn't able to focus clearly on the tasks ahead. In general, the negative effects that a lack of exercise had on my body very quickly started to affect my mind and emotions. The less I was able to focus, the more I found myself escaping into my devices for distraction.

I had to force myself to rediscover movement as part of my daily life because I realized that the benefits far outweigh the time it took for me to do those activities. And it brought me so much joy, too! Movement is not only healthy for our body but also for our mind. Activating our bodies helps with blood circulation, regulates digestion, boosts energy, and improves mood and our overall well-being.

In my early thirties, as I was moving away from competitive ways of moving my body like playing tennis, soccer or basketball, I discovered new ways of movement that do more for me than just improve my physical health. I looked for movement-based ways to improve my mental health, reconnect with the present moment, and support my meditation practice. There were three that stood out as most aligned with that goal.

Practicing Movement: Short Daily Walks

I am sure this next tip won't come as a surprise. Going for a thirty-minute walk daily won't make you a lean athlete, but research has shown that even a brief walk outdoors lowers levels of cortisol, the stress hormone that also deposits fat on your waist and tummy. Daily walks likely won't get you a six pack, but they may reduce your stress levels and prevent some waist fat.

But even more importantly, moving around boosts your metabolism and helps clear your head. More than just clearing it, a brief walk can help to improve concentration, focus, and attention span and is assumed to preserve the health of existing neurons.[128] Having the ability to focus will keep you on-task and away from aimless scrolling. This is why I have made walking a daily routine.

On some days, my walks also include reconnecting with friends. I love deepening my connection with friends while strolling through nature. Other days, my time outside includes mindful walking, which basically means walking while putting awareness on each step and on each breath. It requires more focus, concentration and awareness, so it's probably not something you want to do every time, but I recommend giving it a shot periodically.

Here is what that could look like. Start your walk at a comfortable pace, a little slower than you would normally walk. And pay attention to where you place your feet. Notice the sensation that arises when your foot touches the ground or lifts from the ground. Consciously experience the swinging forward of your feet. Pay attention to your body and how it interacts with the movement and its environment. Shift your attention between your body and the environment from time to time. Notice if there is a wind and what the temperature feels like; listen to the noises around you. Approach the walk with as much curiosity as possible. You can stop at any time, but I recommend at least five minutes at a time of focused awareness on the experience of walking.

Mindful walking has the same benefits as regular walking but additionally creates an improved feeling of well-being, sleep and mood and helps you manage stress more effectively.[129] It's like a short meditation practice that can bring you back to the present moment.

What excites me about my daily walking habit is that it is a chance for a change of scenery, a tiny bit of exploration, and the feeling of the sun on my skin. After every walk, I feel noticeably happier. But most importantly, I get away from my phone and my mind while sinking deeper into my body.

Daily walks are one thing I don't schedule. Rather, I take them when I feel the need to take a break and boost my mood. If I feel antsy with an inability to focus, and a pull to pick up my phone and scroll, it's a signal to me that it's time for a walk. Try incorporating walks into your daily routine when you feel like you need them. Skipping one day is okay. Preferably though, even if you don't have thirty minutes to dedicate to a walk, take five minutes to walk around the block or up and down the street, and notice how much better you already feel.

Practicing Movement: Dancing Ecstatically

Dance is one of the oldest forms of human expression and medicine. It can be a method of social connection, exercise, a leisure activity, and a mental health practice all at the same time. Moving to music has been shown to reduce stress, improve physical health, and be such a strong mental health therapy that it is even used in clinical settings to help treat anxiety, depression, and trauma.[130] It is also a powerful way to recharge and rejuvenate as you untether from tech. Even if you've never really tried dancing, or think you are a terrible dancer, hear me out.

My preferred kind of dance is called ecstatic dance. I discovered this world in 2018. I was skeptical at first, but it has now become an essential part of my recovery practice that improves my mood and ability to concentrate.

> "Ecstatic dance is a form of dance in which the dancers, some-
> times without the need to follow specific steps, abandon them-
> selves to the rhythm and move freely as the music takes them,
> leading to trance and a feeling of ecstasy."

>   - Wikipedia page on Ecstatic Dance[131]

Ecstatic dance is an ancient practice found even in Greek mythology, where its primary effect is described as ecstasy itself. Even back then, it served as a practice of meditation, coping with stress and a general spiritual practice promoting a feeling of connectedness with self and others. Experiencing hundreds of individuals joining together as a community every week to dance wildly and freely has helped me become more connected with myself and my community.

Ecstatic dance organizers create a safe space to dance without talking, drinking, or a nightclub vibe. The first time I tried ecstatic dance, the first moment of dancing in bright daylight without booze or talking was a little intimidating. But after only a few minutes I started feeling the positive energy emitted by everybody in the room. I felt myself letting go of the assumption that people were judging my movement, and I was suddenly dancing more freely than I'd ever done before.

On the Ecstatic Dance website, you can find locations and get an idea of the events they offer and join.[132] And if that doesn't sound like your cup of tea, know that any kind of dance in any setting is great! I'd encourage you to find a dance community where you live that plays the type of music you enjoy.

If dancing in public sounds terrifying, I understand. I'd challenge you to find a private place in your home, turn on your favorite song, and just get moving. It doesn't matter what you look like—you'll feel much better with a clear and free mind afterward. Like the practice of Morning Pages, dancing is a way to release any pent-up thoughts and feelings that are holding you back from being present, which keeps you from feeling the need to escape into your screen.

Practicing Movement: Yoga

The first thing I noticed when doing yoga is how inflexible I am and how difficult some of those positions are because they need flexibility and strength in muscles that I rarely use. But what I did feel immediately after experiencing yoga (besides fatigue and soreness) was a deep sense of relaxation and alignment with my body. According to John Hopkins Medicine, the benefits of a yoga practice go way beyond relaxation and include strength, balance, flexibility, and heart health improvements.[133]

From a scientific perspective, we know that people who practice yoga regularly have higher levels of the amino acid GABA, which people with depression or anxiety typically have low levels of.[134] What is even more interesting is that researchers at the Boston University Medical School concluded that GABA production from yoga was greater than from walking! And similar to walking, it reduced the stress hormone cortisol, meaning that yoga can act as a kind of antidepressant.

But, we don't have to just take it from modern medicine—yoga is both a physical and meditative exercise that has been practiced for over five thousand years for its power to create harmony between the mind and body. I am recommending it as an alternative or addition to some of the practices and techniques described above. Yoga will teach you mindfulness by disconnecting you from your phone and bringing your attention into the body. Through yoga, you'll train yourself to be more present in the moment by focusing on executing the different poses precisely instead of thinking about hundreds of things simultaneously.

The great thing about yoga is how easy it is to get into. You can start right now at home with the Down Dog app,[135] or challenge yourself to find a class in your area! The practice has stood the test of time, so why not try it?

* * *

If you try to eliminate bad behaviors without replacing them with better ones, you're just setting yourself up for disappointment and failure. Calming your monkey mind, creating more awareness, and disconnecting from your smartphone several times during the day will help you recharge your batteries and reconnect with yourself. It will allow you to rebalance the attention from overemphasizing Present You to Future You. Most importantly, it will give you positive tools to replace negative behaviors.

The most effective tool for me in achieving that has been vipassanā meditation. And admittedly, it is the hardest to incorporate into my daily life. That is why having accountability buddies and setting up consequences when failing to do it help tremendously. If you need help setting up your practice or keeping commitments, reach out to me and join the Untethered family at TheUntetheredBook. com.

Also—and this is really important—don't be hard on yourself when you are unable to use all the Reconnect tools every day. The truth is, we are not machines and cannot perform at the same level every day. Instead, look at the tools presented here as "reconnecting deposits." You want to make small deposits every day that accumulate over time to a significant increase in the Distraction Overwhelm line.

You can place deposits by reconnecting with friends, speaking gratitude (arigato), meditating, journaling and moving. On a perfect day you engage in all five at least once. It might help to write down your daily deposit goal in your journal. Here is mine for reference:

Reconnection with Friends: 30 minutes
Meditation: 15 minutes
Journaling: 15 minutes
Movement: 30 minutes
Gratitude Expression: a couple minutes

I know 1.5 hours every day sounds like a lot. And on some days it will be. One of those days, you can combine movement and reconnecting with friends. I really like doing that. Or you can go on meditative walks. If it seems hard to stick to these new rituals, why don't you bring an accountability partner with you on this path toward an untethered life? Making healthy changes together could not only bring you closer to each other but also help both establish new healthy habits.

I am confident that incorporating reconnection with friends, gratitude, meditation, journaling, and movement into your daily routine will be just as powerful for you as it has been for me.

R8: REFRAME

"Over 90 percent of the world's population has an active cell phone account. There's something about technology, in its modern form, that can transcend all cultural, religious, and geographical barriers."

- **Mikey Siegel**, Founder of Consciousness Hacking

We've spent time removing distractions, rearranging our apps and thoughts, repeating new rituals, reducing our smartphone use, and reconnecting to gratitude. We discovered ways to recharge from the daily stresses of being tethered to our smartphone. We incorporated tools into our daily lives that will allow us to be more present, less distracted, and more productive. In summary, we Ranked, Removed, Rearranged and Replaced all of our apps. We began to Repeat new rituals, Reduced toxic smartphone behaviors, Reconnected with a practice of gratitude, and started incorporating practices to recharge without or with minimal use of tech.

Congratulations for taking this untethering journey. This is a good time to thank yourself for the financial and time investment you made to get here. You are investing in becoming your desired future self. Arigato yourself for that.

In this final R, I want to help further improve your digital resilience by expanding your horizon to what is possible when you become untethered and move toward your potential. The two tools in this chapter will help you reframe your ability to achieve success, bring awareness to the needs of Future Me, and help put negative situations into perspective when they arise. They will support you in becoming a marathon runner into your untethered future.

Before I dive into these two mental models, I want to clarify something. We spend hours every day using our devices. But no matter how much time you might spend optimizing your app usage, minimizing toxic habits, or increasing the conscious time spent with your devices, there will be moments when you escape into behaviors that are not fun and don't make you feel proud. This is normal; we are all human, and we make mistakes. When that happens, you can either beat yourself up for your lack of self-control, or you can reframe the situation. Every time you become aware of an unhealthy behavior, you get an opportunity to correct it. And that in itself is progress toward an untethered life.

Gates' Law

"Most people overestimate what they can achieve in a year and underestimate what they can achieve in ten years."[136]

- maybe **Bill Gates**

This quote or versions of it have been attributed to many thinkers throughout the years. You may have seen the same phrase attributed to Tony Robbins, Peter Drucker, or many others. Whatever time span you adjust it to, the gist is that we overestimate what we can do in the short term and underestimate what we can do in the long term.

Two reasons come to mind to explain this phenomenon. First, we are overconfident in our own abilities. Most people think they are better-than-average drivers, better leaders, and able to outperform their classmates in school. This effect is known to scientists as illusory superiority, and it shows up in many fields of life. In a classic study conducted the year I was born (1986), 80 percent of participants evaluated themselves as above-average drivers.[137] In terms of leadership qualities, one study found that 70 percent of the students put themselves above the median.[138] In a study conducted with MBA students at Stanford, 87 percent rated their academic performance as above the median.[139]

This illusory superiority leads us to overestimate what we can do in the short term. Just think about it this way: how often did you wish that you had one more day to prepare for an exam? Just one more day…

So, in the short run, we overestimate our abilities. But studies also show that in the long run, we actually underestimate our performance. In the long run, another cognitive bias outweighs the effects of our own grandiose delusion. This was best described by a University of Colorado physics professor, Albert Allen Bartlett.

"The greatest shortcoming of the human race is our inability to understand the exponential function."

- **Albert Allen Bartlett**

This bias has proven to be true over and over again, and sadly enough, in a recent example. The COVID-19 crisis is a great example of the exponential function and how easy it was to underestimate its wide-reaching effects. On February 29, 2020, news reports indicated there were 70 known cases in the US. A month and a half later, more than half a million cases had been reported in the US alone, and the death toll had climbed past twenty thousand. By the end of 2020, the US had seen over twenty million cases and three hundred fifty thousand deaths, with a variety of lockdowns and protocols put in place to minimize the spread of the virus. The fight against exponential growth was lost in most countries by underestimating what exponentials can do.

Gates' Law states that we tend to overestimate our short-term capabilities and underestimate our long-term outputs. And it doesn't just apply to our own capabilities. In the 1960s, Roy Amara, a researcher, scientist, and president of the Institute for the Future, told friends and colleagues that he believed "we overestimate the impact of technology in the short-term and underestimate the effect in the long run." This effect has become known as Amara's law.

Knowing that this effect exists within the space of technology and human capabilities, how can we use this understanding to reframe our momentary experiences and make sure we set the right goals in the short and long terms? For example, do you need to be so harsh on yourself when you miss an overly eager deadline? How can we establish healthy goals for ourselves while taking these phenomena into account?

Buffered Goals: Putting Gates' Law into Action

One way I incorporate this thinking in my life is through buffered goals. When I plan my week ahead each Sunday, I typically buffer my schedule—I "pad" it a little bit. I know that I might be overconfident in my abilities or think I can achieve more in a week than is realistic.

For example, instead of planning to work for five days in a given week, I only plan to use four days. I try to make the most realistic plan possible by distributing my workload across only four days. Friday is my buffer day. In case I overestimate what I can get done in those four days, I end up working five days. In that case, buffering helps me reduce disappointment because I've still achieved my goals in the same week I'd planned to achieve them. And if I do achieve my goals in just four days, guess what, surprise and delight, I have an unexpected long weekend ahead.

If you have a full-time job during the week and are hoping to work on side projects on the weekend, what would it look like to only plan out goals for Saturday but leave Sunday open? If you manage to get it done on time, amazing; you have a full day of having fun and reconnecting with friends.

I use this technique to get more done in a shorter time frame, but also leave room when it takes longer to work through certain projects. Either way, it increases my chance of success in that week. If I get it done sooner, I have more time for myself or other projects, and if I overestimate my abilities, I have an extra day to make up for it and prevent disappointment.

In terms of achieving long-term goals, I believe that the power lies in consistency, not speed. If we work on our dreams consistently over weeks, months, and maybe years, they will come true. If we achieve our goals every week, exponential growth will elevate us beyond expectations. And although you might not fully believe in it now or don't trust that it will happen, understand that our minds cannot comprehend how quickly things can change and grow. Trust that it will happen as long as you put in the work, consistently. Our devices—like any good partner—are here to support us on this path.

Remember, you are trying to become a marathon runner, not a sprinter. If you are able to consistently and consciously use the time with your devices to achieve your dreams, nothing will seem impossible. If, on the other hand, you get stuck in habitual tech usage loops and let your attention be guided by other parties, your dreams are likely to continue existing only in your head. The choice is yours.

The U-Curve of Happiness

The U-curve of happiness is one of my favorite mental models, partly because it helped me understand why so many experiences I was excited about in the beginning would disappoint me later (and partly because I feel some pride that I discovered it for myself before finding evidence of it in literature!). It describes the relationship between happiness and time when engaging with a new experience.

Let's take language learning as an example. Have you ever tried to learn a new language? If you have, you were probably excited to study a new culture and new ways of expressing yourself initially, only to find yourself exhausted and uninterested just a few weeks later. This type of experience is not something that happens only to you; it's a universal human experience. If you want to know how common it might be, open the Google Doc in this endnote.[140] Analyzing usage statistics at Duolingo, an American language-learning platform with over three hundred million users, reveals that people only complete around 0.1 percent of the language courses they start.

In my experience, happiness over time looks like a U-curve. In the beginning of a new experience, the innocent excitement and fast progress lead to high levels of happiness, until the slow realization that not everything is roses. But after sticking through the valley and learning to appreciate the experience, one comes out on the other side with similar levels of happiness as they felt in the very beginning.

There are many scientific and experiential ways this U-curve shows up. In the Dunning–Kruger effect, people believe themselves to be smarter and more capable than they really are. But more than just being a cognitive bias, the effect shows the relationship between confidence and knowledge that is acquired over time. It proves that people have higher levels of confidence when they have spent very little time acquiring knowledge than when they've spent significant amounts of time doing so. In the middle, when they have a medium level of knowledge, their confidence levels are the lowest.

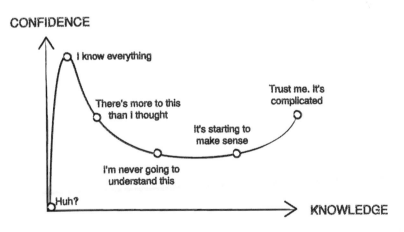

The Dunning-Kruger Effect

In 2008–2009, during the financial crisis, I conducted similar research on the investment behaviors of financial managers while I worked on my first master's degree, in behavioral economics, at the University of Innsbruck, Austria. My professors and thesis advisers, DDr. Huber and Dr. Kirchler, had published a paper just one year before the financial crisis on the value of information in a multi-agent market model. Subtitled "The luck of the Uninformed," it describes a U-curve relationship between knowledge about a subject and investment returns, stating that it gives "a possible explanation why, on average, professional fund managers perform worse than the market index."[141]

It turns out that spending time acquiring more knowledge might not make you more confident in it nor be financially rewarding. Quite the opposite is true. You might go through a long stint where spending more time will make you less confident, less financially well off, and less happy. I am sure this phenomenon partly contributed to how I lost $100,000 on my smartphone. I thought knowing a little more would help me make the right decisions. I was very wrong.

Another way of looking at this relationship between time, knowledge, and happiness is described by an observant mother who noticed how her daughter learned the past tense of the word "go."[142]

When kids first start exploring language, they make progress by taking a few steps backward at times. First, they copy the way their parents and others pronounce the correct form of irregular past-tense verb forms such as "go"/"went," without truly understanding why. Later, they learn that past tense forms are produced by adding an "-ed" to the end of the word. Equipped with that knowledge, they start transforming "go" to "goed" for some time.

Finally, they learn that some words are irregular, and they adjust to the correct past tense form again. Kids basically go from *right and don't know why, to wrong but with more knowledge, to right with full knowledge*. During that same time, parents go from praising their children to correcting them to praising them again, influencing their children's happiness levels in a U-shaped manner.

Or take people who live abroad and often experience stages of cultural shock described by Oberg's four phases model.[143] In the beginning, during the so-called honeymoon phase, they experience high levels of emotional well-being. But as time passes and cultural awareness increases, anxiety and the need to adjust negatively impact the person's well-being. Many months later, during the stage of acceptance, the person can effectively and confidently communicate and interact in the new culture. While they still don't understand everything about it, they have adapted to many of its ways and feel excited about it.

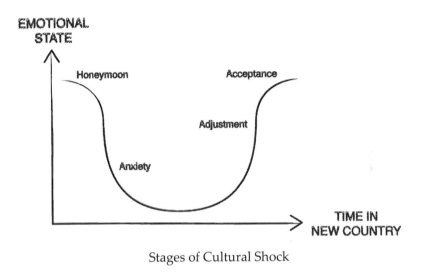

Stages of Cultural Shock

And even life itself seems to progress along a U-shaped curve of happiness. Conventional research suggests that the lowest level of happiness occurs sometime between forty and fifty years old. Of course, it can occur earlier or later.[144] This challenging time has a well-known name: the midlife crisis.

Technology makes it easy for us to quit one experience and jump to another. That allows for a ton of experimentation but also provides an easy escape when something becomes a little less enjoyable. And those times will happen; that is what the U-curve of happiness tells us. If you give up at the point when the curve hits its lowest point, you won't experience how happy the experience might make you later on.

I believe that we have to set our expectations for every experience according to the laws of the U-curve of happiness, always remembering that after the initial honeymoon we will face lower levels of satisfaction. Whether it is a new relationship, work project, or sport we want to learn does not matter. The experience, and your happiness with it, is likely to follow the U-curve of happiness.

This is important to understand because when you feel the low at the bottom of the curve, your devices will seemingly offer you escape from the unpleasantness of reality. But when you give into that escape for too long, you might just extend your low indefinitely. Technology will always be there to take advantage of your weak moments, and it will require an extra level of awareness to make your tech work for you during those times.

When you're feeling unhappy with something for an extended period, ask yourself: "Am I moving toward the flat part of the U-curve of happiness, or is this truly just not a fit for me?" Think about it deeply; meditate over it. In many cases, you will find that there is nothing inherently wrong with what you are doing—you are just on a normal journey. And don't let your devices distract you along the way. Reframe the situation or experience first with the U-curve of happiness in mind before making a quick and maybe costly decision to escape. If you stick with the experience, happiness might be waiting on the other side!

Finally, a word of caution. While the experiences above follow the U-curve of happiness, others seem to behave in opposite ways. Take email load, for example. Professor Monideepa Tarafdar uncovered that emailing is not only a time-consuming activity but can also increase workload stress. Low and high numbers of email load seem to have the biggest impact on stress.

USING THE UNTETHERED TOOLS

In part III of *Untethered*, we talked about tools to prepare your smartphone to be less distracting and more useful for the needs of future you (R1–R4). We then discussed setup guidelines for yourself, your space, and your way of organizing time (R5–R8). By putting the eight Rs into action, you will establish a healthier relationship with tech and yourself and create digital habits that feel nourishing. To help you access and remember what you've learned, the next couple of pages summarize the most important tools and actions from the 8Rs. Look them up whenever you feel the need to revitalize your untethered practice.

R1 (Rank):

1. Utilize the Fulfillment-Based Categorization: Categorize your apps as Unrelated, Desired, Enjoyed, Required, or Hooked.

R2 (Remove):

2. Delete apps in the Hooked and Unrelated categories from your device.

3. Download apps to remove distractions: Brave browser, Forest app, Freedom app, etc.

4. Pay the Happiness Tax: Remove inner distractions by assuming the goodness in others and their best intent.

R3 (Rearrange):

5. Place the apps in the Desired category on a single home screen page.

6. Place the most used and most useful apps from the Required category in the dock.

7. Remove the remaining apps from your home screen (Android and iOS 14+).

R4 (Replace):

8. Identify and replace up to three apps with others that create healthier habits (e.g., YouTube with Audible).

R5 (Repeat):

9. Work with Accountability Buddies: Stay on track by creating win-win situations with friends, and/or use Focusmate.

10. Schedule Time Alone: Schedule your time when you are the only participant and the task takes more than five minutes to do—otherwise, do it now.

R6 (Reduce):

11. Set Up Your Physical Environment for Digital Success: Put away distractions and bring closer what Future You desires.

12. Establish a Morning Routine: Set up your day for success with an established morning routine; try to avoid tech during it or use tech to support the routine.

13. Have a Boring Quiet Hour: invite boredom to foster personal growth.

14. Limit When Your Attention Is up for Grabs: Categorize contacts into three groups (essential, important, and unimportant) and define when and how your time is available. Utilize the "Focus" mode (on iOS) to help you limit when your attention is up for grabs.

15. Reduce Technoference: Avoid using your phone when in person with others. Keep your relationship with your smartphone separate from the relationship with your real-life friends.

16. Put Pride and Joy to Work for You: Identify your distraction danger zone (e.g., 5 pm to 10 pm) and find ways to become more present of your usage during that time. The Yapp Reminders app can help.

R7 (Reconnect):

17. Nourish Friendships: Target at least thirty minutes of reconnection with friends every day.

18. Arigato: Practice gratitude for all the beauty and connection our devices bring to us.

19. Establish a Meditation Practice: Schedule fifteen minutes a day in your calendar. If you need support with your practice, I recommend downloading Oprah and Deepak Chopra's 21-Day Meditation Experience. Give vipassanā a try to deepen the relationship with yourself.

20. Clear Your Mind with a Journaling Practice: Utilize the power of different journals (Morning Pages, bullet journaling) to create clarity in your life.

21. Recharge Through Movement: Practice daily walks, dancing and yoga—they are among the most effective tools to improve well-being, sleep better, and manage stress.

R8 (Reframe):

22. Utilize Gates' Law: Counteract your natural tendency to overestimate short-term outputs and underestimate long-term outputs by buffering short-term goals and having high long-term aspirations.

23. Recognize the U-Curve of Happiness: Internalize the relationship between happiness and time. Often, there is no fixing needed, just a little more perseverance.

FINAL WORDS

On Sunday, March 15, 2020, the Dow Jones plunged nearly three thousand points on concerns about a potential COVID-19 pandemic, making it the third-worst day in its history.[145] Many of us shared fears about the economy and our job security. In the midst of this chaos, my friend Jon Letts published this unusual post on his Facebook page:

I invite you to turn off autopilot

Right now, the world is really fucking scary. It's been easier to live one day at a time than to take a moment of pause and reflect on what really matters [...]

...I'm scared.

I'm also hungry for what we can make of this world.

Our future will come from connecting with ourselves and taking the action we feel drawn to. Trust yourself. I believe in you and whatever it is you're brewing.

I'm asking for you to express yourself in your fullest. Because that's what I and the world need. You to be yourself.

This is not the conclusion most of us might draw during peak moments of fear and crisis. But March 15 was not a normal day by any standard. Within a few weeks of the outbreak, the US went from the best economy in history to hourly workers across most industries having to fear for their jobs.

Prior crises increased income and wealth inequality,[146] and unsurprisingly, this pandemic seems to have hit the already weakened disproportionally, too.[147] Essential workers have been the ones saving our lives by putting theirs at risk. And it saddens me to think that once the stock market returned to growth, it was mostly the ones who had extra cash who were able to profit from it.

One of the other likely results of the COVID-19 crisis is that digital technology has become an even larger part of our daily lives. Many of us are spending more time in front of our laptops and smartphones than ever before. Zoom calls, social media, and online games induced themselves into our daily lives at unprecedented levels. According to McKinsey, "digital adoption has taken a quantum leap" due to the pandemic.[148] As the youngest generation, Gen Z is naturally most open to adopting technological change. They are the first generation to rank "video gaming" (25 percent) as their favorite entertainment activity over "watching TV or movies at home" (10 percent).[149]

The increase in time spent online, reduced physical activity, and the mental/emotional burden of the crisis become obvious when hearing that in the first half of 2020 alone, US life expectancy dropped by a full year, according to the CDC. It is about time that we raise our awareness about overdependence on digital technologies, especially our smartphones.

As my friend Jon so eloquently said:

"Our future will come from connecting with ourselves and taking the action we feel drawn to. Trust yourself. I believe in you and whatever it is you're brewing."

It is time to take full responsibility for your actions and become curious about the world, more than ever before. It is time to take your life in your own hands, away from the distractions of the past. Put fear aside and let go of the anxiety that complexity can bring. It is time to upgrade yourself and allow your powers to emerge. Build resilience to resist the negative media cycle and the lure of extractive algorithms, and be aware of giving yourself too much choice or too many conveniences.

I am asking you to commit to overcoming tech dependency and the distractions that keep you from becoming the person you always wanted to be, the most aligned version of Future You. Part III of this book should have equipped you with the tools you need on this path. It will require commitment, and it will be uncomfortable at times, but it will be the most rewarding experience of your life. Use the eight Rs as your toolset on this journey. Ranking, Removing, Rearranging, and Replacing your apps will only take an hour. This change alone can significantly improve your relationship with your phone.

Make sure to also set up rituals and engage in experiences that help you become more conscious of your choices while incorporating the goals of Future You into your daily routines.

I know how easy it is to give in and start binge watching Netflix or playing computer games all day. I have experienced it myself. If you give in, then do so consciously and with full desire. Enjoy the experience! But don't let the experience take you. Create rituals that serve you, repeat them daily, schedule your own time, and include accountability buddies on your journey. Set yourself and your environment up to reduce unconscious smartphone use, and remember that your smartphone deserves gratitude for its services, too. :)

Just like our devices, we need time to reconnect and recharge our batteries, so set aside time to take care of yourself in this fast-paced world. And finally, know that most experiences will come with ups and downs—maybe even at an accelerated pace due to technology—defined by the U-curve of happiness. Sometimes it pays off to stick with a new experience through the bottom of the curve just to be rewarded with long-term joy on the other side of it.

Being your fullest self and working toward becoming Future You with the help of your upgraded mind, new rituals—and yes, your devices—is not only what the world needs, it is what will make you proud of your life in the long run. Good luck on becoming in the world who you already are in your heart. Good luck in creating your own, untethered life. And if you discover tricks for me to incorporate into mine, I welcome you sharing them with me at TheUntetheredBook.com.

FREE GUIDE

In addition to this book, readers can download a **free, 20-page guide containing 3 clever tricks to master your digital attention**.

Just go to theuntetheredbook.com to get your free guide.

NOTES

1. https://www.digitalwellnessinstitute.com
2. https://core.ac.uk/download/pdf/147643516.pdf
3. https://s3.amazonaws.com/media.mediapost.com/uploads/NielsenTotalAudi enceReportQ12019.pdf
4. https://www.nielsen.com/us/en/insights/report/2020/the-nielsen-total-audi ence-report-august-2020/
5. https://www.qualtrics.com/millennials/ebooks/Millennials_And_Tech_At_ Home_eBook_All_AK.pdf
6. http://www.nature.com/nrn/journal/v12/n11/abs/nrn3119.html
7. http://journals.plos.org/plosone/article?id=10.1371/journal.pone.0030253
8. http://www.nhs.uk/news/2010/11November/Pages/Texting-and-teen-be haviour.aspx
9. https://www.researchgate.net/publication/329666589
10. https://www.harpercollins.com/products/the-teenage-brain-frances-e-jense namy-ellis-nutt
11. Attention economy: a period following the information age defined by human attention as a scarce resource and commodity constantly being targeted.
12. https://www.sciencedirect.com/science/article/pii/S0747563219301153
13. https://www.thegamer.com/15-people-who-have-died-playing-video-games
14. https://www.camh.ca/en/science-and-research/institutes-and-centres/ institute-for-mental-health-policy-research/ontario-student-drug-use-and- health-survey---osduhs
15. https://www.bbc.com/future/article/20180118-how-much-is-too-much-time- on-social-media
16. https://www.thelancet.com/journals/lancet/article/PIIS0140-6736(18)31310-2
17. https://www.reviews.org/mobile/cell-phone-addiction/
18. https://www.nielsen.com/us/en/insights/report/2020/the-nielsen-total-audi ence-report-august-2020/
19. https://www.voanews.com/student-union/generation-z-beats-boomers-spot

ting-fake-news

20. https://www.livescience.com/62220-millennials-flat-earth-belief.html

21. https://surface.syr.edu/cgi/viewcontent.cgi?article=1283&context=etd

22. https://academiccommons.columbia.edu/doi/10.7916/D81N88SJ/download

23. Phubbing: ignoring the person in front of you in order to pay attention to one's phone or other tech

24. Doomscrolling: continuous scrolling or surfing through saddening or depressing news besides the negative impact it has on our well-being.

25. https://www.pnas.org/content/116/36/17753

26. https://www.researchgate.net/publication/336319050_Measuring_complexity

27. https://www.futurelearn.com/info/courses/complexity-and-uncertainty/0/steps/1836

28. https://www.barna.com/research/friends-loneliness/

29. https://www.imf.org/external/pubs/ft/fandd/2020/03/imf-launches-world-uncertainty-index-wui-furceri.htm

30. https://www.vpnmentor.com/blog/online-censorship-country-rank/

31. https://digitalcommons.law.umaryland.edu/cgi/viewcontent.cgi?article=1198&context=fac_pubs

32. https://www.bbc.com/news/magazine-31556802

33. https://www.sciencedirect.com/science/article/pii/S0957417419304270

34. https://www.fastcompany.com/90171429/a-scientific-mystery-why-we-touch-our-phones-even-if-theyre-off

35. https://www.asurion.com/about/press-releases/americans-dont-want-to-unplug-from-phones-while-on-vacation-despite-latest-digital-detox-trend/

36. https://www.forbes.com/sites/kalevleetaru/2019/05/14/sentiment-mining-500-years-of-history-is-the-world-really-darkening/?sh=67e08e8b35ef

37. https://www.psycom.net/negativity-bias

38. https://www.theguardian.com/commentisfree/2018/feb/17/steven-pinker-media-negative-news

39. https://worldhappiness.report/ed/2020/social-environments-for-world-happiness/

40. https://academic.oup.com/sf/article-abstract/98/2/725/5365292

41. https://www.researchgate.net/publication/228280320_Does_the_Internet_ Make_People_Happier

42. https://worldhappiness.report/ed/2019/

43. https://www.researchgate.net/publication/329666589_Unhappy_and_addicted _to_your_phone_-_Higher_mobile_phone_use_is_associated_with_lower_ well-being

44. https://well.blogs.nytimes.com/2010/02/18/how-vacations-affect-your-happi ness/

45. https://bigthink.com/surprising-science/are-people-smarter

46. https://www.bloomberg.com/news/articles/2019-07-29 /how-gen-x-parents-raised-gen-z-kids-different-than-millennials

47. https://www.simplypsychology.org/pavlov.html

48. https://buildfire.com/ios-android-users/

49. https://www.magellantv.com/articles/status-update-how-zuckerbergs-algo rithm-determines-what-you-see-on-facebook

50. https://www.macrotrends.net/stocks/charts/FB/facebook/profit-margins

51. https://www.theverge.com/interface/2019/7/9/20686955/ facebook-groups-border-patrol-anti-vaxx-misogyny

52. https://www.communitysignal.com/the-dark-side-of-algorithms/

53. https://www.humanetech.com/news/newagenda

54. https://www.uscpublicdiplomacy.org/blog/really-dark-side-facebook

55. https://thenextweb.com/google/2019/06/14/youtube-recommendations-tox ic-algorithm-google-ai/

56. https://www.pewsocialtrends.org/essay/on-the-cusp-of-adulthood -and-facing-an-uncertain-future-what-we-know-about-gen-z-so-far/

57. https://www.theatlantic.com/magazine/archive/2017/09/ has-the-smartphone-destroyed-a-generation/534198/

58. https://digitalcommons.salve.edu/cgi/viewcontent.cgi?article=1075&context= fac_staff_pub

59. https://cacm.acm.org/magazines/2009/7/32082-are-we-losing-our-ability-to think-critically

60. https://www.socialmediatoday.com/marketing/how-much-time

-do-people-spend-social-media-infographic

61. https://www.theguardian.com/lifeandstyle/2015/oct/21/choice-stressing-us-out-dating-partners-monopolies

62. https://www.livescience.com/2493-mind-limit-4.html

63. http://webhome.auburn.edu/~mitrege/ENGL2210/USNWR-mind.html

64. https://www.verywellfamily.com/types-of-parenting-styles-1095045

65. https://executive.berkeley.edu/thought-leadership/blog/decision-making-interview-don-moore

66. https://www.livescience.com/2493-mind-limit-4.html

67. https://www.gsma.com/publicpolicy/wp-content/uploads/2012/11/gsma-deloitte-impact-mobile-telephony-economic-growth.pdf

68. https://www.nielsen.com/wp-content/uploads/sites/3/2019/04/the-quest-for-convenience-2.pdf

69. https://www.usatoday.com/story/money/2019/05/07/americans-spend-thousands-on-nonessentials/39450207/

70. https://www.finder.com/cost-of-convenience

71. https://www.nationalgeographic.com/news/2018/05/plastics-facts-infographics-ocean-pollution/

72. http://maristpoll.marist.edu/wp-content/misc/usapolls/us180423_NPR/NPR_Marist%20Poll_Tables%20of%20Questions_May%202018.pdf

73. https://www.walkersands.com/resources/the-future-of-retail-2019/

74. https://time.com/5324940/americans-exercise-physical-activity-guidelines

75. https://www.businessinsider.com/us-life-expectancy-declined-for-third-year-in-a-row-2019-11

76. https://www.cdc.gov/nchs/data/vsrr/VSRR10-508.pdf

77. https://advances.sciencemag.org/content/5/1/eaau4586/tab-figures-data

78. https://www.pewresearch.org/social-trends/2020/05/14/on-the-cusp-of-adulthood-and-facing-an-uncertain-future-what-we-know-about-gen-z-so-far-2/

79. https://journals.sagepub.com/doi/pdf/10.1177/2056305120912488

80. https://tlexinstitute.com/how-to-effortlessly-have-more-positive-thoughts/

81. https://mutta.dhamma.org/dhamma-discourses/be-self-dependent/

82. https://psycnet.apa.org/record/1982-22772-001

83. http://www.cell.com/neuron/abstract/S0896-6273(14)00804-6

84. http://www.buffalo.edu/news/releases/2002/12/5996.html
85. https://greatergood.berkeley.edu/article/item/six_surprising_benefits_of_curiosity
86. https://www.amazon.com/Top-Five-Regrets-Dying-Transformed/dp/140194065X
87. https://www.zippia.com/advice/average-number-jobs-in-lifetime
88. https://www.businessinsider.com/why-you-get-sick-of-your-favorite-song-2016-6
89. http://www.nytimes.com/2010/08/25/technology/25brain.html
90. http://www.nytimes.com/2010/11/21/technology/21brain.html
91. https://journals.aom.org/doi/10.5465/amd.2017.0033
92. https://convers-ate.medium.com/what-is-a-jeffersonian-dinner-758fa0a3a55
93. https://qz.com/887010/netflix-nflx-launched-streaming-video-10-years-ago-and-changed-the-way-we-watch-everything/
94. https://www.rhyslindmark.com/marriage-counseling-with-capitalism/
95. https://topics.amcham.com.tw/2019/10/garbage-island-to-recycling-model/
96. https://brave.com/
97. https://www.forestapp.cc/
98. https://freedom.to/
99. https://www.flipdapp.co/
100. https://offtime.app/
101. https://apps.apple.com/us/app/channel-control-your-apps/id1464464213
102. https://www.getintention.com/
103. https://www.hidefeed.com/
104. https://www.hidelikes.com/
105. https://ma.tt/category/in-my-bag/
106. https://psychcentral.com/blog/the-golden-rule-of-habit-change#1
107. https://www.newyorker.com/magazine/2019/10/28/can-brain-science-help-us-break-bad-habits
108. https://www.statisticbrain.com/new-years-resolution-statistics/
109. https://www.apa.org/topics/willpower-limited.pdf
110. https://www.focusmate.com/
111. https://www.flow.club/

112. https://www.calendar.com/blog/how-to-color-code-your-calendar-for-optimal-success/

113. https://jamesclear.com/three-steps-habit-change

114. Technoference: interruptions in interpersonal communication caused by attention paid to devices

115. https://reincubate.com/camo/

116. https://www.autopilot.ooo

117. https://www.sciencedirect.com/science/article/pii/S0747563216303454

118. https://apps.apple.com/us/app/yapp/id1437096658

119. There are many great videos online describing how it works in detail. Here is a short example: https://www.youtube.com/watch?v=fm15cmYU0IM

120. https://www.fastcompany.com/90171429/a-scientific-mystery-why-we-touch-our-phones-even-if-theyre-off

121. https://www.vox.com/science-and-health/2019/8/1/20750047/millennials-poll-loneliness

122. https://journals.sagepub.com/doi/abs/10.1177/1745691614568352

123. https://chopracentermeditation.com/article/6-oprah_deepaks_21_day_meditation_experience

124. https://www.dhamma.org/en-US/courses/search

125. https://www.youtube.com/watch?v=DNwp_nysiik

126. https://www.youtube.com/watch?v=ixu4Kd5R1DI

127. I've also tried writing with friends every morning, which worked really well for accountability. If you need a more dedicated tool, I recommend 750words.com. Either way, choose an accountability tool that you can commit to.

128. http://www.psychologytoday.com/blog/do-the-right-thing/201202/Does-walking-make-you-smart-yes-and-in-more-ways-you-think

129. http://www.arthritistoday.org/what-you-can-do/staying-active/walking/walking-meditation.php

130. https://www.google.com/books/edition/_/Q-OFSEeeI5UC?hl=en&gbpv=1

131. https://en.wikipedia.org/wiki/Ecstatic_dance

132. https://www.ecstaticdance.com/

133. https://www.hopkinsmedicine.org/health/wellness-and-prevention/9-bene

fits-of-yoga

134. https://www.ncbi.nlm.nih.gov/pubmed/17532734

135. https://apps.apple.com/us/app/yoga-down-dog/id983693694

136. https://fs.blog/2019/05/gates-law/

137. https://doi.org/10.1016%252F0001-4575%252886%252990004-7

138. https://archive.org/details/selfsocialjudgme00alic

139. https://www.jstor.org/stable/3090112

140. https://tinyurl.com/4wwcxc6j (created by Duolingo user Maxinator10000)

141. https://link.springer.com/article/10.1140/epjb/e2007-00046-2

142. https://www.bridgetofarabia.com/blog/2012/03/u-shaped-curve-of-develop
ment.html

143. https://www.youthreporter.eu/de/beitrag/are-you-depressed
-or-are-you-just-experiencing-the-culture-shock.14813/

144. https://link.springer.com/article/10.1007/s10902-016-9830-1

145. https://www.cnbc.com/2020/03/15/traders-await-futures-open
-after-fed-cuts-rates-launches-easing-program.html

146. https://hbr.org/2018/09/research-how-the-financial-crisis
-drastically-increased-wealth-inequality-in-the-u-s

147. https://www.wsj.com/articles/covid-upended-americans-finances
-just-not-in-the-ways-we-expected-11609081200

148. https://www.mckinsey.com/business-functions/strategy-and-corporate
-finance/our-insights/how-covid-19-has-pushed-companies-over-the
-technology-tipping-point-and-transformed-business-forever#

149. https://www2.deloitte.com/us/en/insights/industry/technology/
digital-media-trends-consumption-habits-survey/summary.html